Eatonfield
Things to do

1/ Arrange meeting with
2/ Send another letter to B
3/ look at structure of Grove
4/ Write speech for presentation
5/ Sales team meeting drive sales
6/ KM PW & Re London trip - funds
7/ Check with Steve Jones re: Birkwood Planning
8/ Address cash flows with PM
9/ Agree contract with Paul Brett
10/ Put offer in for South Coast Shopping centre
11/ Chase Brendon Flood up re Paignton
12/ Wales Busram Installer check date
13/ See DH about Retail Portfolio
14/ Go through deal with Barry Owen
15/ Get all info off Larry
16/ Ian Arnott - Workington Tony Cunningham MP
17/ Endorse Baker Tilly Audit
18/ Diner - Gordon Mackennan
19/ Flyer - Kirsty to circulate
20/ Need to see Evolution
21/ Lunch with David Armitage - Re: Plan
22/ Foxy Fearnall - variation
23/ Ian Roberts - presentation @ Buckley
24/ meet Jill Jones
25/ Savilk inspection

RAISING THE BAR

Rob Lloyd

Matador
5 Weir Road, Kibworth Beauchamp
Leicester LE8 0LQ, UK
Tel: (+44) 0116 279 2299
Email: books@troubador.co.uk
Web: www.troubador.co.uk/matador

ISBN 978 1848761-599

A Cataloguing-in-Publication (CIP) catalogue record for this book is
available from the British Library.

Book Cover & interiors designed by Wise Monkey Design & Media
Front cover photograph - ©Matthew Seed Photography
Inside front cover photograph - Phil Micheu
Back cover photograph - Carrie Davenport
Inside back cover photograph - Dave Cooper

Printed in the UK by TJ International, Padstow, Cornwall

Matador is an imprint of Troubador Publishing Ltd

CONTENTS

This book is dedicated to Winston James Lloyd, known to me as Sam, who died in January 2008 aged 68 and Margaret Alice Lloyd who died a year later, both of whom inspired me to work hard, aim high and never give up.

Sam gave me one of the most valuable assets I have which is a good education.

Margaret was a constant, loving presence in my life.

I will always be grateful to them; my father and my grandmother.

FOREWORD

'Never give up.'

In 1990 I was twenty-six years old, I had a house worth a quarter of a million pounds, I drove an £18,000 Jaguar and I was the owner of a very profitable company, Lloyd Property Investments Group (LPI). I was making money like there was no tomorrow and I was flying high, running the business of my dreams. My personal life was going well too; I was married to Jan and we had a two year old son, Jason and another baby on the way. I was a lucky man with everything to live for and on target to fulfil the goals I had first outlined for myself seven years ago at the age of 19; goals that I'd wanted to achieve by the time I was 30:

To run a profitable business
To be a millionaire
To marry a beautiful woman
To own a house with a long drive and a snooker room
To send my children to public school

To drive a Bentley

To stay in the best hotels in the world

To own my own racing yard

To give something back by donating to charity

To train a Grand National winner

And with the confidence of youth I had no reason to suspect I wouldn't achieve it. I was working 12 hour days in pursuit of my dream with absolutely everything to live for. I was a good negotiator, focused and ambitious and as my father, Winston Lloyd, used to say: I never gave up. Once I saw the possibility of a deal I went for it. Perhaps it was all too much too soon, who knows? But what I do know is that less than five years later it was all gone. By 1994 I'd lost everything; my business, our home - and the Jaguar.

Our son, Jason was now seven years old, our daughter, Joanna was five and Daniel was nearly three. I could barely scrape enough money together to put down a deposit on the rental of a two bedroom caravan in a field in North Wales, never mind a house. As for my dream of owning a racing yard; the only horses I was looking at were the ponies in the field next door.

I remember the winter of 1994 vividly. My wife and I were sitting in the caravan with frost on the inside of the windows, the wind whipping across the adjoining fields and whistling under the door.

"We can't go on living like this much longer," was all she

could say as Daniel slept in the cot next to our bed.

I had no job and not one asset to my name. This was not how I had envisaged my future six years ago and I couldn't help wondering how on earth this had happened. Had I simply raised the bar too high?

From the age of three I spent most weekends learning to ride at Lodge Farm where my great grandparents, Mary and Teddy West lived. By the age of eleven I was pretty good in the show jumping arena and I remember my Uncle Bill watching me as I put my pony Cogshall Rocky through his paces attempting a clear round. Uncle Bill was visiting my parents at Flash Farm in Cheshire where we all lived. For every two of the four foot high fences I cleared, I knocked one down; for every three I cleared, I'd fall off and tumble onto the grass.

Uncle Bill was my dad's uncle. Not only did he ride with the Shropshire Hunt, he rode in the 1958 Grand National and if anyone was going to give me tips on how to get over fences it was him. I wanted a clear round and I wouldn't stop until I'd achieved it, so every time I fell off, I'd just get back on and try again. It seems that Uncle Bill was impressed.

"Young Robert's got what it takes to be a good farmer, Winston; he never gives up," he announced once we were back at the farmhouse later that day.

And my father looked at Uncle Bill and said confidently: "Rob's not going to be a farmer, Bill; there's no money in farming any more. But you're right; he never gives up."

And I remember feeling both pleased and puzzled at this pronouncement. If I wasn't going to be a farmer, then what was I going to be?

By 1998 I was well on the way to rebuilding my business, not just back to where it was but bigger and better than before. In November 2006 I floated Eatonfield on the Alternative Investment Market, AIM, and released £5m cash as well as an additional £10m for growing the business. I then had the wherewithal to establish my own racing stables, Rob Lloyd Racing, and I had begun to think about devoting time and energy to charity.

I think the story of how I got back in the saddle is worth telling.

CHAPTER ONE

Horses are in my blood

'There's a fine line between fearlessness and recklessness.'

One of my very first memories is of helping my parents with the potato harvest at Nook Farm where I grew up. It was 1967 and I was only three years old at the time, so this wouldn't have involved much more than sitting on my dad's lap while he drove the tractor. Dad's full name was James Winston Lloyd but for reasons I can't remember I always called him Sam. To everyone else he was known simply as Win.

Nook Farm was a dairy farm but Sam had been supplementing his income for a few years by growing potatoes which he harvested and sold to the local potato merchant. What I didn't know was that he was already putting some of this money aside for my education. Perhaps if I'd known about his plans for my future I would have paid a bit more attention.

On this particular day I was sitting on the stacked bags of potatoes as they were loaded off the harvester when I lost my balance and fell under the machine. I can still see Sam's horrified face as a drill disc continued to operate and sliced across my left foot.

It was obvious within moments of hitting the ground that my foot was badly damaged but I didn't appreciate just how serious the injury was but if my parents had not reacted as quickly as they did I would probably have been riding side saddle for the rest of my life.

Sam scooped me up off the ground and shouted to my mother to get in the car and then driving as fast as he could we headed for Northwich's Victoria Hospital.

Victoria Hospital is still there today. There are only 31 beds in the whole place; tiny by any hospital's standards but to my young mind it was the scariest place in the whole world.

My mother clutched me as tight as she could, still wrapped in the sodden blanket, worried that if she relaxed her grip for one minute the blood would drain from my foot and I'd lose the limb. Meanwhile, I was strangely calm. There was something about Victoria Hospital that I found comforting and reassuring; it was the smell of the antiseptic, it reminded me of Nook Farm; more specifically it reminded me of Sam's scrupulous cleaning of the farmyard.

As the nurse examined me I was comforted by the fact that if the hospital cleaned their floors as often as Sam cleaned the yard then no harm could come to me. He wasn't afraid of hard work; as far as he was concerned there was never any substitute for it when it came to pursuing your ambition. And he's right of course; whether it's growing potatoes or putting together a multi-million pound property deal, it's hard work that gets the deal done.

"You'll have to take Robert to Altrincham General," said the nurse, sounding as if she was in a rush. "The foot needs specialised care and attention. The ambulance is waiting outside, Mr Lloyd. Take him through straight away. Quickly now."

At the age of three I had no idea how serious the injury was, all I knew was that I was doing most little boys can only dream about: I was sitting inside a speeding ambulance, lights flashing, as we sped across Cheshire, to south Manchester.

I didn't lose my foot, although Lloyd family stories retold on high days and holidays say it was a close run thing. All I know is, I was in hospital for a couple of months and had to have a painful operation to knit the wound with skin taken from the top of my thigh and grafted on to my foot. The scar is still there today, in fact it looks as if my foot has been zipped back on.

I'm not sure what this vividly recalled episode taught me about life. Perhaps it was nothing more than a harsh lesson to be more careful when sitting around watching the potato harvest. But I know what it didn't do: it didn't stop me taking risks - in business or otherwise - and it certainly didn't stop me sitting on a horse, or worry about falling off one. I couldn't wait to get my first pony and it wasn't long after I got out of hospital that my great grandparents, Teddy and Mary West introduced me to Flicka.

Flicka was a calm, black beauty, 11hh and completely bomb proof. Teddy and Mary, my mother's grandparents, lived at Lodge Farm, Norton near Runcorn and that's where Flicka spent most of her short life. My great grandparents made a living by growing crops, mainly turnips, and by breeding turkeys. Even today, I can still recall the rancid smell of the blood of a slaughtered turkey as it's hung upside down, throat slit, in preparation for Christmas - Grandad West's busiest time of the year.

The rest of the land on Lodge Farm was rented out to local owners of horses and ponies, which was heaven as far as I was concerned. I spent every moment I could making a fuss of Flicka and enjoying the fact that all the stable girls who worked there made a fuss of me.

I specifically remember Carol Hayes who treated me as if I was her own lucky mascot. I suppose I must have looked quite cute in my jodhpurs and little riding jacket and it was Carol who taught me to ride. By the time I was four I was pretty competent, completely fearless and totally hooked on horses in a way that all young boys seem to get hooked on their own particular hobby, whether it's trains, football or making model aeroplanes. We live and breathe our obsession and, as far as I was concerned, Flicka was my obsession.

At weekends I would be up at seven, I'd bolt down my breakfast, which was always cooked by Nan West and invariably included a fresh egg laid by one of the hens in the yard; I would pull on my jodhpurs then dash out to see Carol and Flicka. Carol would put me through my paces, watching me go from walk to trot to canter. If I was performing well she'd let me have a go at a few jumps. I always wanted to jump higher than she wanted me to but I knew even then that there was a fine line between fearlessness and recklessness - something I've realised is true for most things in life, not just riding horses.

Even now I can remember the feeling of accomplishment, practising in the fields at Lodge Farm. It was the challenge that excited me because I wasn't competing at this stage; I was simply trying to improve.

But those idyllic days in the mid to late 60s were marred in my mind by what happened next.

Flicka was happily cantering in one of the fields when she got her foot stuck in a rabbit hole. Grandad West realised as soon as he examined her that there was nothing they could do. He made the difficult but humane decision that she had to be put down.

Nan West told me what had happened and I was inconsolable. But she knew there was only one way to get over the loss; she decided within a few weeks of Flicka's death that I had to have another pony.

So within a week or two Teddy and Mary introduced me to Crispin. Crispin was also black with a white star on his forehead, 11.2hh and the perfect second pony in every way. As soon as I jumped up in his saddle and pressed my heels into his flanks it felt right. Crispin was the first pony that I competed on.

I think it might be helpful at this stage to describe just how much horses meant to the Lloyd family. My grandfather, Jim Lloyd farmed with shire horses and although his son Sam didn't enjoy riding he always encouraged my love of the sport and, as part of the farming fraternity, we all took an active interest in the hunt.

But it was Sam's uncle, William A Roberts, known in the family as Uncle Bill, who took riding to another level.

Uncle Bill was a great supporter of the Shropshire Hunt and often rode out with them. In 1958 he competed in the Grand National on his hunter, Princess Garter. Unfortunately, to the disappointment of the whole family, Princess Garter was brought down by another horse and failed to finish.

This event took place six years before I was born but it was thanks in part to Uncle Bill that I began to compete in the show jumping arena. In fact, if I wasn't riding Dobbin the rocking horse in Nan West's living room and winning the Grand National myself in the final straight, I was outside in the fields practising my jumping.

From the ages of six to 12 I competed in various gymkhanas on a succession of ponies; first Crispin, then Junior, then Silver.

Most weekends I'd leave the comfort of my bed at Lodge Farm and head for the stables to clean the pony's tack while Carol plaited the horse's mane and tail; then I'd tuck into a full English breakfast, pack the lunch Nan West had prepared and then load my pony into the horse box. My mother or Carol would drive us to the competition and we would stay all day.

Meanwhile, 20 miles away, Sam was working all the hours God sends building up his dairy farm into a viable business. He'd paid £14,000 for Flash Farm in 1971, after selling Nook Farm which had once belonged to his father, Jim. Jim had died young leaving Sam to manage the day-to-day running of Nook Farm at the age of 15.

My father was helped in this mammoth task by his mother, Margaret Alice Lloyd, a formidable business woman who died this year at the age of 98. In recognition of her skills in accounting and administration our family farming business has always been known as 'M A Lloyd & Son'. Unfortunately, her husband, Jim was better known for his drinking and gambling.

Sam however was both ambitious and conscientious and put those attributes to good use as a farmer and also as a husband when he married my mother Pamela in 1963. Pamela was just 18 and already pregnant with me when they tied the knot but by all accounts it was a genuine love match and they were very happy, at least for the first ten years or so.

Unfortunately, by 1976, things took a turn for the worse. In 1976 Pamela left the farm forever, running away with the man who'd constructed the new silo tower at Nook Farm and Sam never really recovered from the shock.

I was completely unaware of these gathering storm

clouds because I was too busy competing at gymkhanas and winning rosettes, notching up a couple of hundred in total before I'd hit my teens. A local newspaper report in 1976 lists me as the winner of the most points in the under 12 category at the horse of the month show at Penyffordd in North Wales and by now it was clear to most people who knew me that I was enjoying the winning as much as the riding.

It was also around this time that I had my first big betting win. Nan West liked a flutter and used to place a bet nearly every day, often slipping me a five pound note with the instructions "Don't tell your mother!"

The excitement and thrill of claiming £9 on Red Rum's first Grand National win in 1973 was, for me, probably as fantastic as Red Rum's trainer, Ginger McCain, winning the greatest steeplechase in the world for the first time. How could anyone forget the gutsy Australian champion, Crisp, battling it out with local hero Red Rum in the punishing final straight?

Crisp was carrying the top weight of 12 stones, but he was jumping superbly. At one stage he was 25 lengths clear and it looked as if no other horse in the field could possibly catch him but then with two fences to jump, he began to tire.

I remember reading years later that Crisp's jockey, Richard Pitman, said he made the 'classic schoolboy error' of picking up his whip and as a result his horse veered left and lost three lengths, effectively losing the race. I'm more inclined to believe it was the fact that Red Rum just never gave up.

As the horse crossed the finishing line all I remember feeling was sheer exhilaration; it was as if I was sitting on Red Rum myself, head and shoulders above the crowd.

By now I was also riding out with the Cheshire Forest Hunt, often with my cousin Paula in tow. Paula was a couple of years younger than me and a pretty good rider in her own right but I used to treat her like a younger sister, in other words I ordered her around and made her do what I wanted. There was one particular meet when we were galloping as fast as we could, struggling to keep up with the bigger horses, me on my piebald wonder, Cogshall Rocky; the horse that could jump anything (or so I thought) and Paula on Silver. One of my good friends at Antrobus C of E Primary School was Keith Shore, another keen horse rider and now an international show jumper with a farm at Crumleigh Heath near Northwich. It was Keith's father who sold us Cogshall Rocky for £600, which was a huge amount of money at the time.

Paula and I hadn't been riding long when I took a cracking tumble into a ditch and had to wait a good five minutes with my pony on top of me before being rescued. Fortunately Cogshall Rocky and I were both unharmed so I got back in the saddle and urged him on, determined to catch up with Paula before she could claim victory and tell the tale to whoever would listen.

Looking back on all this it's easy to see where I got my

love of horses and it makes perfect sense that I should want to make them part of my life in years to come although at this stage I was more focused on a career as a show jumper. But it's difficult to have a successful career as a show jumper unless you have plenty of money or an indulgent sponsor and I had neither of those things. What I did have however, was a good education.

CHAPTER TWO

Sport and camaraderie at Rydal

'I was beginning to understand how important it was to be part of a team.'

I wasn't a particularly academic student but that doesn't mean I didn't like school. I really enjoyed the years I spent at Rydal Penrhos in Colwyn Bay, North Wales. I boarded from the ages of 11 to 16, captained the Rydal rugby XV and football team at the age of 13 and played an influential part in the cricket and tennis teams. I may have taken seven attempts to pass my English 'O' level but I didn't need telling twice by Sam, or anyone else, that I should make the most of a good opportunity.

In 1972, when I was eight years old, a report from my state primary school, Antrobus C of E, said that I needed to spend more time practising my reading and advised my parents to allow me to read as much as I wanted. The problem was; I couldn't sit still long enough to pick up a book. I'd get bored and want to move on to something else; a characteristic that seems to have stuck with me to this day.

Three years later, Gordon Weir the Head Teacher at Antrobus stated on my reference for Rydal that when it came to games and PE I was *'keen and thrusting' and that 'I wanted to succeed'*. I was also, apparently, a popular boy.

So, it was looking promising that I would be accepted. Sam had been to a fee paying school too - although he spent a lot of his time attending local cattle markets instead of lessons. Nevertheless he was convinced of the advantages of a good education and I didn't disagree, it's just that on the day that we were discussing my application I was preoccupied; I had something to confess and I didn't know where to start. I remember sitting next to him as he drove me home from Nan and Teddy West's at Lodge Farm and in the end I just blurted it out:

"Sam, I've been stealing from you."

He looked at me quizzically. "Have you? What have you taken?"

I took a deep breath. "I've been stealing your ball bearings from the work shop."

"And what have you been doing with them?" he asked.

"I've been playing marbles. Did you know that ball bearings are classified as 'goggers'? I've been beating everyone else. I beat Billy Bates last week and took all his goggers. He wanted them back of course, so I charged him."

"And how much did it cost Billy Bates to get his goggers back?"

"A couple of pounds," I said sheepishly.

Sam said nothing, but I got the distinct impression that he didn't completely disapprove. He might even have made a comment about me having an eye for a deal.

I also fancied myself as a bit of a card sharp with Three Card Brag a favourite game of mine. I have both my grandmother, Margaret and Nan West to thank for that.

At the age of 10 they would take me to their local whist drive in Daresbury where I'd sit with their friends and join in the games. The problem was; I was so good that more often than not I'd win, picking up hampers and bottles of whiskey in the process. Nan and Grandma would treat me to a fish and chip supper on the way home and then I'd pass my winnings on to the rest of the family.

I believe the other members of the whist drive eventually complained, saying I was far too young to be part of their group, although I suspect they resented me because I kept winning rather than the fact I was only 10 years old. After that I had to content myself with playing cards at home with the family. Except I wasn't content, because my Uncle Frank Banner was better than me and would regularly take all the money I'd just earned selling back marbles to my mates. He's also only a couple of years older than me and more like a brother than an uncle - with all the competitiveness that entails.

Uncle Frank was my mother Pam's step-brother and we spent a lot of time together as children. It was thanks to him that I realised I was a particularly bad loser, often sulking for hours when he beat me at cards and it was also thanks to Frank, many years later, that I decided to pursue a career in property.

Given the close knit nature of my family I'm always amazed at just how quickly I settled into life at Rydal. I think it was partly because there was so much to do there; I had no time to feel homesick and given my inclination to keep busy, I thrived. It was also a place that encouraged ambition and where the masters got to know you as individuals.

Once I'd dragged my trunk over the threshold of the dorm on that first day in September 1975 I never looked back. My mother and Sam hugged me briefly and then left to begin the 60 mile journey back to Flash Farm while, in an initially hushed atmosphere, I and seven other boys concentrated on unpacking our belongings.

It was during my first term at Rydal that I met Giles Richmond. Giles became a good friend and was best man at my first wedding but it was my colleagues in the rugby team who became my partners in crime.

By the time I was 14 I had grown to my full height of 5ft 6ins, well built with muscles honed on the rugby pitch and tennis court. As sportsmen we obviously all thought we were 'the business' and that it was unreasonable to wait another four years before we could legally buy alcohol; we looked older than we were, surely someone would serve us?

There was one particular Chinese restaurant in the town of Colwyn Bay that we discovered would serve lager, as long as we ordered food at the same time, so we would put on our best swagger, wander in and order a bowl of rice. We never ordered anything else from the menu - just the rice - and then the waiter would bring us a couple of beers.

While I was testing the rules outside school, I was knuckling down and working hard when I was within Rydal's four walls. Sport was my passion and I remember Ken Jones my geography teacher putting me forward as captain of the football team. Even though I wasn't the most academic pupil he saw a determination in me that he encouraged. I was getting reports with comments such as *'If industry were the only criteria for success, he would surely pass'* (history) and *'He has worked hard and deserves to succeed'* (physics) but no-one could claim that I was setting the academic world alight. I struggled in English, often managing to *'miss the point'* and in commerce, apparently, I *'always managed to take the long way round.'*

To be honest, I find my commerce teacher's statement the most surprising. Today if there's a speedy way to do business, I'll find it. In 2006 my company, Eatonfield, bought the Bookham Technology Site in Paignton, Devon for £5m. Months later we sold it on for £10.075m, which by anyone's standards must qualify as taking the quick route to success.

On the sports pitch however things were fast and furious. In 1978 Rydal's school magazine, *'Experiment'*, printed a match report that stated I had given my utmost *'vocally, physically and eventually by example'* and that I'd *'contributed more than anyone else to the team's successes'.*

I repeat these statements here, not because I want to blow my own trumpet, but to highlight a characteristic that was beginning to develop in me the longer I was at Rydal. I was beginning to understand how important it was to be part of a team; the success that I wanted in life didn't just come from the exertions of one individual but from the efforts of a group of people and it was that lesson, more than any other that I learned at boarding school. Unfortunately I didn't always apply that principle when I was running my first business, LPI. But by the time I'd set up Eatonfield in 1998, I'd learned my lesson and I made sure I surrounded myself with people I could trust as well as the best advisors that money could buy.

Still pushing the boundaries, I soon moved on from the occasional pint of lager to a disastrous experiment with vodka. Another colleague and fellow pupil, Phillip Arundale and I were celebrating the end of term exams and we downed a whole bottle between us. Unlike me, Phillip wasn't a boarder and made the sensible decision to leave me and go home, while feeling distinctly queasy, I found my way to the squash courts. I threw up everywhere and was discovered by my house master, Mr Pitman who naturally ordered me to clean up my mess, which I did, without another word.

I remember feeling both embarrassed and disappointed with myself and years later I had the same sensation after a night out in Chester. After meeting up with colleagues, I'd downed one too many beers at a time when my first business was in trouble. I was living at Bricklecroft, my £250k house in Cheshire with my wife and three children, Jason, 5, Joanna, 3, and Daniel, 18 months, as well as Sam and his mother, Margaret. I can't remember why I'd been drinking but I'm guessing I was worried about the state of the property market and attempting to relieve the stress the only way I knew how. I'm not making excuses for myself, but all I did in those days was work; I never had time to do anything else.

Sam watched as the taxi dropped me off outside the front door that night in 1992 and waited until I'd put my key in the lock, then he walked into the hall to meet me.

"Where have you been?" he asked.

"Out," I said, trying to push past him towards the stairs.

"Well, you're late. Have you forgotten you've got a wife and three children?"

"No, of course I haven't," I slurred. But of course they had been the last things on my mind while I'd been out having a good time.

"You should know better," said Sam and at that moment I saw red. I don't know if it was because he was telling the truth or that I was simply petrified at the realisation that the property market was falling into recession and taking LPI with it. All I know is that moments later we were brawling on the front lawn, tumbling out of the house to get a better swing at one another.

Sam traded punch for punch. It didn't matter that he was

24 years older than me and a slighter build; he gave as good as he got, with neither of us holding back. I lashed out and landed a punch on Sam's chin, he hit back and I felt the full force of his clenched fist against my cheek. Neither of us wanted to back down and I dread to think how much more damage we would have done to each other if I hadn't been drinking.

The following morning we sat in silence at the breakfast table. We were both sporting bruises and black eyes. I don't know if the women of the house were disappointed with me, but I certainly was.

Next thing I knew, I was reaching across the table and holding out my hand. Sam stretched his hand out to meet mine and we shook solemnly. I ached all over and my head was banging fit to burst but one thing had sunk into my thick skull; nothing is as important as family. You don't turn your back on those you love and who love you and you certainly don't let them down through stupid, inconsiderate actions like staying out all night when they need you.

"We'll say no more about it," said Sam and we never did.

Strange as it may seem, we developed a mutual admiration after that night. Growing up on the farm I'd never been as close to Sam as I was to my mother, probably because he had always been so busy working, but overnight I became a big fan of his quiet, steady approach to life. He had not had an easy time over the years. When his father died Sam was only 15 and he had to take over the running of the almost bankrupt Nook Farm. He managed to turn it around through sheer hard work, later selling it and buying the bigger Flash Farm only to have my mother leave him five years later. By that time I was away at school and he never remarried. He always had his own mother living with him of course, but I don't think that really filled the void.

When my mother left Flash Farm she went to live with her new partner in County Durham and she and I met up only once in the next 12 months. I wasn't too happy that she'd started a new life without us, in fact I was furious and that's when my grandmother, Margaret stepped into the breach. Margaret became a big influence on me over the next few years and I've often wondered if I inherited my love of business from her. But Sam didn't really recover; he was never the same again. When my mother left he lost interest in the farm and it went steadily downhill, slowly going from bad to worse.

By the late '70s running Flash Farm as a profitable business was becoming more and more difficult, Sam was drinking quite heavily and he eventually took the decision to sell up. He and my grandmother then moved into The Croft; a large family home in Kelsall and bought Smithy Garage in the village of Comberbach where they carried out MOTs and general servicing and sold new and second hand cars.

It was around this time that Sam started to have a serious relationship with one of the ex-milkmaids at Flash Farm; Isobel Parry. She was a lot younger than Sam, probably only six or seven years older than me in fact, and she wasted no time in getting what she wanted out of the relationship. She moved into The Croft and insisted that Sam build a large extension on the property which I knew he couldn't afford. I was at school with her brother, Edward, so it wasn't as if I could ignore what was going on at home; Edward was there to remind me.

Sam and Isobel were together for a number of years and looking back, I'm pretty sure she took him for a ride financially. But there wasn't much I could do; I was away at Rydal, and Sam was a grown man. I didn't worry about him and I doubt very much that he worried about me. I was independent and keen to make my mark and I concentrated on doing just that both in term time as well as during the school holidays.

I remember one year the opportunity for a school skiing trip came up. I was so busy playing rugby I didn't get the chance to practise on the dry slope but, even so, I managed to persuade Sam that it was an opportunity not to be missed and he allowed me to join pals Phillip Arundale and Giles Richmond for a week in the Pyrenees.

Phillip and Giles had had a whole series of lessons in preparation for the week's skiing so they were fairly competent. They knew how to snow plough and seemed to have no trouble stopping. In my opinion, it all looked pretty straight forward; I was convinced I could ski just as well as they could, even though I'd never been on a pair of skis in my life.

So, on day one I pushed off from the top of the slope, attempting to follow them as they executed parallel turns all the way down the mountain. But I shot off far too fast and within seconds I was completely out of control, I couldn't stop and crashed into the side of the mountain, losing a ski in the process. I was fortunate I didn't do myself some serious damage.

The next morning I was covered in bruises but, true to form, I was back on the slopes with the two of them, determined to give it another go. Sam's favourite phrase was probably ringing in my ears: "He never gives up!"

Unfortunately I no longer ski or play rugby due to a back injury a few years ago. But I still manage to ride now and again and I play tennis whenever I get the chance.

In 1981 I passed five 'O' levels; English literature, art, maths, craft and design and religious studies. Sam had sold the farm the previous year and now owned the garage in Comberbach and he was having difficulty paying the school fees. I had to leave Rydal: it was time now to make my own way in the world.

CHAPTER THREE

An eye for a deal

'If you give me a chance I won't let you down.'

Sam advised me to get a trade under my belt and since he'd now sold Flash Farm and was running the garage he suggested I train as a mechanic. But even as I enrolled at Chester College in the autumn of 1981 I knew this was not what I wanted to do. I think it says it all when I say that the only thing I can remember about the course was that I managed to sell a car to one of the lecturers for £400. Even then it seems I had an eye for a deal.

Uncle Frank was now training as a surveyor in London with National Car Parks (NCP) and he told me that the property industry was full of opportunities for someone with ambition so I immediately began writing to local estate agents, enquiring about a position as a trainee negotiator, sending off what seemed like hundreds of applications. No-one offered me so much as an interview until Warrington Borough Council eventually called to discuss a position in the Estates Department. Unfortunately, my lack of an

English Language 'O' level was a big problem since the position was dependent on the successful applicant studying for a degree in surveying and valuation and students had to have the 'O' level to be eligible for the course. Luckily for me the council decided to take a chance and I was offered the position, on the understanding that I pass the exam at the next attempt. If I failed, I'd lose the job.

I'd also recently met Jan Williams in Tiffany's nightclub in Chester. By all accounts she liked my determination and self-belief and I remember telling her I was manager of Sam's garage when, in fact, I was no more than a grease monkey.

So, here I was, a few months after leaving school in Colwyn Bay, living with Sam and my grandmother, Margaret at The Croft in Kelsall, commuting 15 miles to work in Warrington every day and then 20 miles in the opposite direction in the evening to see Jan. I don't know if the travelling was to blame but in January 1982 I failed my English 'O' level for the sixth time. My manager's hands were tied and I had to leave the position within the Estates Department. Warrington Council said it couldn't create a precedent and had to stick to the rules.

Many years later, my negotiations with planning departments only confirmed my belief that if there's a council rule in existence, no matter how impractical or unreasonable it appears to be, it will be rigorously applied - to the letter.

Once again at the age of 18, I had no job. In London,

Frank's career as a surveyor was going from strength to strength and so I decided to widen the net and apply for jobs further afield.

In 1982 I applied for a position with Wilson's Estate Agents in Oxfordshire and was called in for an interview with one of the partners, Mark Baker. The first interview went smoothly and I was invited back for a second.

I remember sitting in Mark's office and trying to persuade him that he should offer me the job. I was caught in the old trap where if you had no experience you couldn't get a job, but if you had no job you couldn't get the necessary experience.

Mark looked down at my CV and asked me the question I knew he'd ask: "Why should I offer you this position, Rob? You've got no relevant experience and you're a long way from home. Why should I take a chance with you?"

I looked around Mark's office which was situated in the centre of the market town of Witney. I remember it as quite a pretty place with its own sense of history, not quite as much history as Chester perhaps, but still interesting in its own right. There was a market square, a 17th century town hall and the 13th century church of St Mary just around the corner in Church Green. It had a high school, Henry Box Comprehensive, which was named after a local boy who, like Dick Whittington, had travelled to London to seek his fortune. In 1662 the successful Mr Box left enough money to found a school in his own name. Who knows? Perhaps Mark Baker would find the prospect of a young man travelling from Cheshire to Witney to make his fortune an interesting comparison?

"If you offer me the job I won't let you down," I said, looking Mark straight in the eye. "I'll show you how good I can be if you'll just give me a chance."

And that's exactly what Mark Baker did. In 1982 I became a commercial assistant at Wilson's Estate Agents, Auctioneers, Surveyors and Valuers at 32 Corn Street, Witney and I worked hard to keep up my side of the bargain.

Mark was an inspiring and encouraging boss as well as a bit of a character. He was 6ft 2ins, very witty and fond of repeating phrases such as 'Stuff a stoat' and 'f*** a ferret', which I think was his own way of saying 'well I never'. He referred to his PA as 'Shagnasty', which fortunately she took to be an affectionate rather than a cruel nickname and he often made the joke that he'd taught me everything he knew in just a week. He was being modest of course; he knew a lot more than I could pick up in seven days, I was just keen to learn. Besides, there are some things you can't teach. There are times when you have to trust that your judgement is the right one, even if you appear to be swimming against the tide. That level of confidence only comes with experience and at this stage in my career that's exactly what I didn't have.

Mark was also keen for me to study for the Incorporated Society of Valuers and Auctioneers (ISVA) at the college of Estate Management in Reading but the lack of the English

'O' level raised its ugly head yet again. So, I sat the exam for a seventh time convinced that if I failed this time I would have to give up once and for all.

During the two years I spent in Witney I didn't have time for horses, in fact the only sport I found time to take part in was snooker. I was working long hours and commuting back to Cheshire regularly but I'd discovered a snooker hall just down the road from my bedsit. When I wasn't studying for exams I'd spend most evenings there, chatting to the girls on the reception desk and taking on anyone who fancied a game. In my usual, addictive way I won more often than I lost, with the whole experience bringing back memories of a wonderful family holiday in 1975.

I was 11 years old when Sam announced that we would be spending a week at The Hotel Bristol in Newquay.

It wasn't long after we checked in at the reception desk that I spotted a fantastic, full sized snooker table and persuaded Sam to join me for a game. I was immediately hooked and it was pretty obvious to both of us that I would have been quite happy to play snooker with Sam all day, every day and never leave the hotel. The only problem was; it was popular with the other guests too and as an 11-year-old boy, I wasn't going to be allowed to take precedence over everyone else staying at The Hotel Bristol even if I was playing with my dad.

I had to think of a way round the problem and the only solution I could come up with was to visit the snooker room when no-one else wanted to play.

So, for the rest of our holiday I knocked on Sam's bedroom door at six o'clock in the morning and listened to his groans as he got ready to join me downstairs. He didn't want to get up early because a) he was on holiday and b) he'd usually had a skinful in the bar the night before.

Looking back now, I'm not too sure if it was the game of snooker I loved most or the fact that I was getting Sam all to myself – not an easy task when your dad's a farmer. Either way I will always remember that week in 1975 as one of my most enjoyable and memorable holidays for two reasons; I played snooker for a couple of hours before breakfast every day with Sam and I came up with one of my very first ambitions: I decided that when I was a successful businessman I would buy myself a house with a room big enough to hold a full size snooker table.

But back in 1982 my ambition was stalling slightly thanks to the fact I didn't have that necessary English 'O' level certificate, which was a real hindrance since in all other respects I was doing well; Mark Baker was impressed with my ability and the effort I was putting in at Wilson's. When I sat the English exam that summer I had no idea if I'd hit it right this time, but I knew that if I didn't pass I wouldn't be able to move on to my ISVA qualification.

Fortunately for me, seven was my lucky number and I finally got the qualification I needed. I went on to the College of Estate Management in Reading and 12 months later I was looking for another challenge. It made sense to come back to the Northwest so in 1984 I applied for a job with a local estate agency, the name of which I won't reveal for reasons that will become clear, suffice to say, this particular agent is still doing business today.

I was offered the position I applied for and duly handed in my notice at Wilson's but the job was subsequently retracted when I was told that a relative of one of the partners had now been offered the position instead. I was forced to go back to Mark Baker and ask if I could have my job with Wilsons reinstated. To my surprise and relief he said yes.

Then in 1985, when I was 21 years old, I was offered the position of manager at Thomas C Adams Estate Agents in Denbigh, North Wales. It was also the year that I decided to get married.

By the time Jan and I walked down the aisle at Bagillt Church, I'd moved on again to Grimley and Son in Manchester.

As Office Agency Negotiator at Grimley's I switched from residential property to commercial and a whole new world of opportunity opened up for me. After dealing with buildings worth thousands of pounds in the estate agency business I was now looking at office and retail premises worth hundreds of thousands, sometimes millions, of pounds.

One of my first big responsibilities was the Piccadilly Plaza development in the centre of Manchester where Grimley's was joint agent. This was a 2.5 acre site, comprising retail, leisure and a massive office tower, the first mixed-use, purpose built development in the city which still dominates the skyline today. I helped to negotiate 95% occupancy of the building, arranging flexible leases and offering deals with incentives for tenants. It was also during this phase of my career that I met Nick Leslau.

Today Nick Leslau is Chair and Chief Executive of the privately owned Prestbury Group which has assets totalling £3b including hotels, hospitals, Madame Tussauds and Alton Towers, but in 1983 at the age of 23 Nick was MD of the Burford Group. This was the year he negotiated to buy the unloved Piccadilly Plaza from Eagle Star and appointed Grimley's to help refresh the tenant mix, becoming a tenant himself in the process.

Burford sold the rejuvenated Piccadilly Plaza in 1988 for just under £20m and immediately became an inspiration to me. In 2008 Nick appeared in the third series of *Secret Millionaire,* giving away more money than any other individual before or since – including me!

Before getting married, I'd invested in the property market on a personal level. In 1983 I bought a two bedroom bungalow in Bagillt, North Wales for £25k and with the help of my in-laws paid an extra £10k for two-and-a-half acres of adjoining land. Two years later, having obtained planning permission for 12 more bungalows, I sold the plot for £50k to Graham Finch, a Chester-based businessman and owner of a very proactive company called Homelink, paying back my in-laws in the process.

Graham and I exchanged contracts on the land but

unfortunately he wasn't able to complete straight away so I allowed him more time until he could. Once he'd got the money together Graham went on to sell the two and a half acres for a decent profit to Warrington's plc and as a 'thank you' for my patience, invited me on an all expenses trip to Portugal for the grand prix. We stayed in a top hotel next to the casino with some other friends and ate in the same restaurants as James Hunt and Murray Walker. It was like a Rydal school trip all over again, but with more money and worse behaviour! Married or not; I couldn't wait to go back.

It was around this time that I met another local businessman, Peter Stevenson. Peter was a consultant with Allied Dunbar who'd contacted me regarding insurance matters. We got on well; it was obvious to me that Peter was entrepreneurial and had some interesting contacts. I was sure we could do business together.

Meanwhile Sam's cousin, John Lloyd, was involved with the owners of a property called Warren Hall which was situated at the gateway to North Wales and he told me there was the chance that the owners, Pioneer Holstein Breeders were looking for a buyer. Peter and I expressed an interest and wasted no time in lining up a buyer of our own: Parchester Ltd, in Birmingham. If the sale progressed smoothly, Peter and I calculated we would make £1.75m on the deal - each.

In anticipation of the big pay out Peter and I arranged to test drive a Rolls Royce at Henley's in Chester and as we climbed into the car I remember having this fantastic feeling that I'd actually made it at the ridiculously young age of twenty-one, nine years before my deadline.

But within a week the deal went completely cold and for Peter and me it was back to much more mundane matters, like paying the mortgage. But I sometimes wonder how different my life would have been if the deal had gone through. Who knows, I might be running a much bigger property company by now, or I might have fallen much harder than I did in 1994 and struggled to pick myself up again.

With the money I received from Graham Finch from the land sale I then bought a large, double-fronted detached house in Chester for £49k. I remember Jan saying we couldn't afford the mortgage repayments and she was right, we couldn't – on our own, but there was a self-contained flat in the property which we rented out to a young IT professional called Mike. Mike lived with us for two years, paying our mortgage in the process.

By late 1986 I'd decided it was time to move on from Grimley's and I applied for a position as a surveyor with NCP. Frank had been in touch again and hinted that there was a job available and I didn't need prompting twice. I applied and was called for interview.

All in all, 1987 ended up being a pretty eventful year: I was offered the job as a trainee surveyor with NCP and I was given my first company car; a gold-coloured Ford Escort. I also became a father for the first time at the age of twenty-three.

But just weeks later I thought my career with NCP was over before it had even begun when I crashed the Ford Escort on the first day I drove it. Fortunately Jason's arrival into the world was much smoother and calmer. I loved being a dad, not just because I welcomed the responsibility but also because it helped me focus even more on what I wanted out of life, both for me and for my family.

Today I drive a Bentley, or should I say; my chauffeur Paul Ditchfield drives my Bentley. Jason, or J as I call him, is twenty-one years old and the MD of The Waterstown Club. I couldn't have wished for a better outcome on both counts.

CHAPTER FOUR
Onwards and upwards –
and all the way back down again

'I realised that I wanted a bit more input into the future of these developments; I wanted more control.'

In 1987 I was 23 years old and married with one son. I was working hard, travelling around the country for NCP, on the lookout for suitable commercial sites that my employer could develop.

We were now living in a double-fronted detached house in Halkyn Road, Chester and I was earning £14k a year, which wasn't a fortune by anyone's standards but wasn't bad for a trainee surveyor. Thanks to our tenant, Mike, who was living in the self-contained flat in our house, we were able to afford the bigger mortgage, which at £49k had stretched us to the limit financially.

I knew it wouldn't be long before we added to our family and I was more than happy to be the main bread winner; it's just that while I was working in that role my wife's ambitions didn't always coincide with mine. She was still keen for me to stick with the 'steady job', while I was focussed on those 10 goals that I'd formulated at the age of 19:

To run a profitable business

To be a millionaire

To marry a beautiful woman

To own a house with a long drive and a snooker room

To send my children to public school

To drive a Bentley

To stay in the best hotels in the world

To own my own racing yard

To give something back by donating to charity

To train a Grand National winner

I still had seven years before my deadline which, at the age of 23, I considered plenty of time. Working at NCP was giving me invaluable experience when it came to finding suitable sites for commercial development and I was travelling from Manchester to Birmingham to Newcastle in the process. I was involved in all sorts of deals; I was working on the management of an office block at Birmingham airport at the same time as helping colleague, Nigel Hunter in Newcastle and enjoying some raucous nights out on the town when I was there. But even though I loved every minute of it, I knew that if I stayed with NCP the opportunity for achieving my personal ambitions was minimal so, when I saw the opportunity to move on again, I took it.

This time the advertised position was for a land buyer with David Mclean Homes in Flintshire, North Wales which was probably one of the biggest turning points of my career.

David Mclean was, until recently, one of the largest house builders in the UK with a turnover, at its peak, of £280m. In October 2008 the company filed for administration, not just because banks were unwilling to forward credit, but because of two specific incidents. The first blow came when the company suffered a bad debt and irrecoverable work in progress totalling almost £300k; the second was when work was halted for 26 weeks on a site in Liverpool where David Mclean was the main contractor. A Polish worker was killed when the crane he was operating collapsed underneath him, his cab crashing on to the partly constructed building below.

After a lengthy investigation the Health and Safety Executive concluded that there was not enough evidence to prosecute, but the damage had already been done. The combined effect of these two incidents meant that in May 2007 David Mclean lost a total of £6.1m. The house building arm of the company has since been sold in a management buyout, rumoured to have cost the new owners £40m, and is now trading as Elan Homes but there were enough painful redundancies along the way to create a significant hole in the employment figures of Flintshire for that year.

I wanted to mention all of this as a timely reminder of how things can turn bad so quickly. In 1993 when my first company, LPI Group ceased trading it was also due to very specific problems and not just to the looming recession. Of course, I lost tens of thousands of pounds rather than millions of pounds and there were three reasons I could pinpoint for my company's demise, rather than two. But the end result is the same; misery and despair for everyone concerned.

In 1988, however, the property industry was buoyant and it looked as if there was only good news on the horizon. David Mclean decided I would be more useful, not as a land buyer for residential property but, building on my experience at NCP, as a dealmaker for commercial developments. David Mclean made it clear that it was interested in back-to-back deals and wanted me to find suitable sites to sell on: they told me they were not interested in building a portfolio.

The arrangement that was suggested suited us both at the time. David Mclean proposed that I be appointed a director of a new division of the business to be called Enterprise Developments. I would be responsible for setting up and running Enterprise Developments for which I would be rewarded with a 25% stake in the company.

I welcomed the challenge and wasted no time in completing the first deal in my new role; buying an old roller skating rink in Warrington. As director I negotiated to buy the site, obtained planning permission for offices and subsequently sold the development on to the Refuge Insurance Group. David Mclean made £350K on the deal.

Another roller skating rink, in Preston this time and with

a nightclub attached, was bought and sold without planning permission, also for a healthy profit.

It wasn't long before I was being offered opportunities that David Mclean was simply not interested in. They had no desire to use their own money to buy sites, they wanted the banks to fund their buying and then move quickly on to the next deal. I realised that I wanted a bit more input into the future of these developments; I wanted more control. So at the end of 1989 I set up my own business, LPI.

By this time we'd had another baby; Joanna, known as Jo, born on 27th November and I decided it was time to upgrade our living accommodation.

The next three years was a roller coaster of activity. I bought a pair of semi-detached properties near Dodleston, Cheshire and immediately set about converting them into one large family home with enough room for Sam and my grandmother, Margaret to move in with us. I don't remember any opposition from Jan at the thought of having to live with both her father-in-law and her grandmother-in-law but I think the thought of having help on hand with a young family was too good an opportunity to miss. I wasn't often around and although I thoroughly enjoyed being a dad, I felt my responsibilities lay more with providing for the family financially. I wanted my children to get a good education and as far as I was concerned that meant going to public school. Besides, I knew that I was much better at building a property business than I was at coming home at 5pm every night.

The LPI Group started life at the kitchen table of our new

home and it took off straight away. Even though later in that same year interest rates nudged 15% I wasn't too worried. I was busy and I was ambitious and nothing was going to hold me back; I had a small mortgage on Bricklecroft which was now worth about £250k and I was driving a Jaguar. It seemed as if I could do no wrong. At the age of twenty-five I'd had no real experience of failure although plenty of experience of hard work and as I've always believed; the key to success is hard work.

I don't often analyse what it is that I do well, but I think part of my success is due to the fact I know a good deal when I see one and I know when to sell. I always strive to add value to a development and to leave something behind for the purchaser. At least that's what I know now. In 1990 things weren't quite so cut and dried, thanks to the three problems I was about to experience – all at the same time.

The first development that was to cause me difficulty was in Station Road, Colwyn Bay. This was a freehold property I'd bought in the North Wales town I knew so well, not a million miles from my old school Rydal, opposite Boots the Chemists. I converted the ground floor into a pub, the Sir Robert Peel, and added residential units on the first floor, with the regular income from the pub tenants effectively paying for the conversion work. Unfortunately, the tenants went bust within a year or so, which of course, then had serious knock-on effects for the rest of the development.

In Prestatyn high street I'd bought another commercial property at about the same time, renting out the ground floor to both a butcher and an insurance brokerage and converting the upper floor into offices and flats. I remember that one of the businesses renting a first floor office was a publisher of a magazine entitled *Afloat,* which was ironic given that the magazine sank without trace within 18 months.

The third development to cause me serious concern was a once derelict shop in Pwillheli which I had completely renovated. Once again, the tenant's business got into difficulty and they defaulted on their rental, making this the third disaster for me in one year. Of all the businesses renting property from me at the time, only one survived; the butchers in Prestatyn.

By now Dan had been born and LPI had started to default on its own loan repayments. I was called in to see manager, Eric Jones of Lloyds Bank in Chester.

As soon as I entered his oak-panelled office and saw Eric's face I knew this was not going to be an easy meeting. In fact, it was worse than I anticipated.

"This is a difficult time for businesses like yours, Rob," he said, looking worried.

"I know," I replied. "And you've been incredibly supportive to me over the last three years, Eric, but I'm sure that things will improve in the near future. It's just that with these punishing interest rates everyone in business has to reassess their situation."

He looked at me with an expression that told me nothing. But I wasn't naïve; I realised that Eric must have had his own manager breathing down his neck and he would be expected to do something about the situation pretty quickly. Extending my loan didn't appear to be one of the choices on the table.

"I admire your ability to take risks, Rob, but I feel that your luck may have finally run out."

I stared at him as the full meaning of what he was saying began to sink in. I know Eric viewed me as a maverick; I know he found my youth and relative inexperience quite hard to deal with but I also knew that as a bank manager of the old school he valued our relationship. He didn't want to force me into bankruptcy any more than I wanted to be declared bankrupt.

"Give me a week," I said, trying not to think of my family. "I'll come up with a solution that I hope you'll find acceptable. I promise I'll come back in seven days, Eric, and I'll figure out a way to make sure you get what you want."

And I kept my promise, but as I walked out of his office that day in May 1993 I knew the only solution that would satisfy the bank was going to involve selling everything I owned.

As I walked back to my car I thought of that proposition and how it would affect my family. How was I going to tell them that we would have to sell our house? And what about Sam and Margaret; they would be losing their home too.

By the time I pulled up into the drive at Bricklecroft the

full impact of what this would mean for us became all too clear. I realised I had the ability to come up with a solution that the bank would find acceptable but I had no idea what my wife would think. No, that's not true; I knew exactly what she would think. She would hate it

"How did it go?" asked Jan as she held Dan in her arms. She was looking at me carefully from the open kitchen door as I walked down the hall towards her, six-year-old J alternately hopping up and down and clinging to my leg, happy to see his Dad at this hour of the day.

"As expected, I suppose," I said, avoiding her gaze and immediately set about working out the value of my assets.

By the time I went back to see Eric Jones seven days later I had a detailed plan of how I was going to get out of this mess. In short, I was selling everything. I put the house on the market with Strutt and Parker, estate agents in Chester and arranged local agents to market the commercial properties in North Wales. I think Eric appreciated the gesture because even after liquidating all my assets there was still the issue of paying the outstanding Lloyd's bank fees. I don't know if he took pity on me or if he was just relieved that I'd paid off most of the debt thereby making his own position relatively safe but, either way, he decided to write off the final £3k.

As I left Eric's office I realised I had lost everything I'd built up over the last few years. I was back to square one. I had no home, no source of income and no real potential for earning a living. Fortunately I had my family, my health

- and my car. But after a few days in a B&B I realised I would have to sell that too. The money from the sale meant I could put down a deposit on somewhere to live.

The two bedroom caravan I subsequently found as our temporary home was sited in a field in Halkyn, North Wales. It was used as a holiday let and was owned by a couple called Muriel and Tommy but they took pity on me and allowed us to live there indefinitely, in fact we were there for a full two years in the end. By the time we'd moved in and paid the deposit as well as the first few months rent I was down to my last £50. It wasn't long before that went too.

The winter of 1993 was particularly memorable and for all the wrong reasons. It was freezing cold and there was condensation dripping like rain on the inside of the windows. I remember my wife making scones when we had no money for bread and I couldn't help comparing this time to a year ago when I was drinking Champagne in the wine bars of south Manchester.

Even worse was the attitude of my previously very supportive father-in-law, Alan Williams. When LPI had been on a high, Alan had assured us that if things ever took a downturn then he was there for us. But I only ever remember the offer of a hot bath being made once, even when we had no hot water in the caravan. Meanwhile Sam had to rent somewhere to live and Margaret moved in with her daughter, Gill, in Widnes, where she would remain for the next 18 years of her life.

Looking back, I wonder if those two years in that damp, miserable environment taught me something. I'll never forget the kindness of Tommy and Muriel, for example, or the actions of David Williams, an architect and colleague I'd worked with occasionally on my LPI properties. He heard of my situation the following year when, just as I was getting on my feet having bought a clapped out car and with work just starting to trickle in, I had a few drinks in Chester and decided to drive home to Halkyn. When my wheel clipped the curb of a narrow bridge as I drove over the River Dee I was stopped by police. It was obvious that no amount of pleading by me was going to persuade the officers to let me off, but nevertheless I tried. Short of giving them my life story there was no way they'd understand how important a car was to my future employment prospects. I needed to drive; no-one was going to entertain a property professional if he couldn't.

The irony was, I had just been celebrating my first property deal in two years with solicitor and friend Keith Mather and was looking forward to an upturn in my fortunes at long last. They listened politely but charged me anyway and I ended up with a two-year ban.

Christmas of 1994 was when I honestly thought things could not possibly get any worse. David Williams heard of my predicament and drove over to Halkyn with toys for the children, a frozen turkey and a bottle of wine.

As we sat eating our donated Christmas lunch I wondered if this was the final straw, not just for me but for my marriage too. Living in a caravan with no job and no money is not ideal. It occurred to me that this might be putting our shaky relationship through one test too many.

CHAPTER FIVE

Starting again from scratch

*"I need to know that anything I buy today I can
sell tomorrow at a profit.'*

It was now the early-90s and the country was going
through a recession, dragging me with it. We were living in
a caravan in a field in Wales, I had no assets and no job but
I did have a wife and three children to support and we had
to live somehow.

There was a pawn shop in Brook Street, Chester, just half
a mile from the house we used to own in Halkyn Road and
I became a regular visitor. ,

Even today I find it difficult to describe the feelings of
shame and humiliation as I crossed the threshold of that
pawn shop; I was so embarrassed but I simply had no
choice. I couldn't borrow from Sam as he had very little to
his name himself having sold the garage in Comberbach
years ago. My grandmother, Margaret, needed financial help
and I knew Sam could do without me adding to his burden.
Plus, I couldn't help feeling guilty that both of them had

had to leave their home when I sold Bricklecroft.

So that's why I pawned the gold charm bracelet that my mother had given to Jan a few years ago and that's why I also pawned the sovereigns that Margaret had given to us as an investment. I even pawned my wife's engagement ring. We had no credit cards; there was nothing else I could do.

After visiting the pawn shop I would walk into the city and pace the streets, telling myself that things would get better and trying hard to be positive. To be honest, I didn't always succeed and there were some days when I admit I felt sorry for myself. But at least I was keeping out of everyone's way and not having to come up with a different answer each time Jan asked me why I didn't have a job. The children weren't suffering as they were too young to treat living in a farmer's field as anything other than an adventure but I knew they didn't like it when their mum and dad argued. It was best for all of us if I simply wasn't there.

In 1994 there were quite a few homeless people on the streets of Chester, which is shocking given that Cheshire is a relatively prosperous county. I don't know if it was because of my own situation that I became so interested in theirs but it seemed as if we had a cross section of society living rough; from middle aged men with stooped postures who'd obviously been on the road for years, to teenagers who looked as if a gust of wind would blow them away. It wasn't so much the older tramps I felt sorry for but the youngsters, often with a skinny dog in tow, sitting on the cold, damp pavement with an upturned hat or an outstretched hand asking for spare coppers. I wanted to help and I wanted to know how they'd got into this terrible situation; living rough with nowhere to wash, have a decent meal, or a warm bed to sleep in. Coming from a close knit family like mine it was impossible for me to have any real concept of how different these youngsters' lives were. It was hard to tell if they were ill or if they'd just run away. Perhaps the reality was their family had thrown them out onto the street?

I didn't ask any of these questions because I wasn't in a position to help and besides, part of me felt that I was only a step or two away from the same situation myself.

But there was also something about the hopelessness of the expressions on these young people's faces that made me feel fortunate to have as much as I did; it put everything in perspective. I don't mean that I felt superior to them, far from it, because deep down I admired their fortitude and the fact that like me, they weren't giving up. The sellers of the *Big Issue* in particular; what they were doing was exactly what I had been doing until recently: running a business. It just goes to show that with a bit of help a homeless person can earn an income that could eventually help them get off the streets. It was just getting that initial boost that was the difficult bit.

It was while I was thinking about all this that I stumbled on an idea to make some money. At this stage I hadn't had my driving ban imposed, in fact I didn't have a car. Fortunately for me lots of other people did and I knew there would always be a market for a car park in the centre of Chester that was safe, secure and cheaper than the multi-storey car parks currently on offer.

I noticed a collection of Budget Car Rental vans parked on a patch of waste ground at the back of Habitat, just off one of the main routes into the city and realised straight away that it would make more money as a car park than a storage depot. Chester, like many other old established towns and cities, is not built for easy access and parking is expensive. There is a park and ride system in operation on the outskirts of the city but, given the choice, many visitors still prefer to drive into the centre.

This particular area of waste ground was in a good spot, central for both shoppers and office workers so I tracked down the owner and persuaded him to lease his land to me for 12 months.

Within a couple of days I'd put a garden shed at the entrance to the site, bought an old cash till, a book of raffle tickets and erected a sign charging far less than the multi-storey around the corner. I also made a point of asking drivers to leave their car keys with me so that I could move the vehicles around and squeeze more into the available space if I had to. On busy days I managed to fit 120 cars into an area that was really only big enough for 100 vehicles. I worked 12 hours a day, seven days a week and although I wasn't earning enough money at this stage to move my family out of the caravan it still felt good to be clawing my way back up. That is, until one particular Saturday afternoon when a former colleague drove his Land Rover Discovery into my car park.

Richard Baddiley couldn't hide his shocked expression when he saw me but he was far too polite to ask what I was doing sitting in a wooden hut in the middle of a car park in the depths of winter and I was too embarrassed to explain the situation, so we just nodded at one another while I took the keys to his £30k vehicle and tried not to think of the Jaguar I had been driving 18 months ago. If there was ever a moment when I felt the weight of failure pressing down on my shoulders then this was it. It really brought it home to me, looking at Richard, that some people were surviving the recession - and I don't just mean keeping their head above water, but actually thriving in the difficult economic climate. That feeling I had when I was younger of losing at cards, or not getting a clear round in the show jumping ring or watching another team win on the rugby pitch hovered over me like a big black cloud and I hated it. Deep down I knew I had the ability to win again, but sometimes hard work just isn't enough; you need a bit of luck too. I kept telling myself that tomorrow was another day and if I didn't give up then luck had more chance of finding me. And six months later, I'm relieved to say that it did.

Today, from time to time, Richard Baddiley works for my property company, Eatonfield, but if you'd told me that in

1994 I don't think I would have believed you.

The hours I spent sitting in that old shed weren't wasted; I would scan *Estates Gazette,* the property developers' bible, looking for opportunities around the country, reminding myself that I had once been well known as a dealmaker. I'd been renowned for my network of contacts, whether it was with liquidators, receivers or private individuals and I was convinced that there had to be just as many opportunities for bargains in the property world now, from sellers desperate to offload a development or from those keen to trade up, as there had been in the past. It was just a matter of finding the opportunities and persuading someone else to put up the cash for the initial purchase. I didn't have any money of my own to put into a deal, so I aimed to work on a commission basis once I'd sold the development on.

My wife and I were like ships in the night at this stage but, as far as I was concerned, I had no choice but to keep working these long hours. By now, I was starting to earn money and I'd even managed to buy back everything I'd pawned over the last 18 months.

I'd also scraped together enough money to buy an old car because I knew I had to travel further afield to find the sort of deals I wanted. It was important to be there, on the ground, available to negotiate when the opportunity arose, so Sam offered to take over from me in Albion Street on the days I needed to be somewhere else.

I was still in touch with Uncle Frank Banner, of course.

His career in London with NCP was going well and when he saw me he would occasionally slip me a couple of quid to tide me over.

I was travelling up to London quite regularly now, on the look out for opportunities, although I didn't dare put my old car through the punishing 400 mile round trip so I took the train and, I'm ashamed to say, hid in the toilet when the guard was doing his rounds. Once I'd arrived at Euston station I'd go straight to Frank's office, where he'd buy me lunch then I'd visit the site I'd come to see and take the train home later that day, once again in my own private compartment.

I knew exactly what I was looking for; anything I could buy then sell on quickly at a profit. I also developed a reputation for quirky deals; by that I mean messy developments that I would buy, tidy up and make institutionally acceptable before selling them on again at a profit.

Then in 1995 I landed the big deal that finally got me back in the market as a property developer but was also the cause of my driving ban.

I'd spotted a site that I felt was suitable for NCP; a derelict plot in Cardiff that I managed to turn around quickly and make a healthy profit of £75K. It's difficult to find the right words to describe the sense of achievement once the deal had been done; suffice to say, it felt fantastic! I celebrated in some style with old friends, one of whom was Keith Mather.

We eventually found ourselves in the Duke of Westminster owned Grosvenor Hotel in Chester city centre. The Grosvenor is the only five star establishment in the city and has a Michelin starred restaurant, which in those days was called The Arkle. I don't think many people outside of the horse racing fraternity would know that Arkle, a three times winner of the Cheltenham Gold Cup, was recently voted the winner in a poll of all-time favourite racehorses seeing off both Red Rum and Desert Orchid. It's 40 years since Arkle won his first Gold Cup but his achievements have stood the test of time. As well as his Cheltenham treble, he also won the King George VI Chase, the Irish Grand National and two Hennessy Gold Cups. Such was his class that when running in handicaps he was forced to give away huge amounts of weight - yet still managed to come home in front.

In his 34 races he carried at least 12 stone in 23 of them but finished with a career total of 27 victories. And the reason the restaurant was named after him? He was owned by Anne, Duchess of Westminster.

So that's where I started my celebrations. I finished them on Chester's Handbridge, half way across the River Dee, talking despondently to a police officer.

The prospect of letting my recent achievements slip through my fingers was not an option for me even though I now had a two-year driving ban. I was on the right track to get the family out of the caravan and I couldn't afford to lose the initiative but I couldn't build on my success unless

I had transport.

By now, the 12 month contract on the car park in Albion Street was coming to an end which meant, on the one hand, that the regular income I was receiving was about to finish, but on the other, it meant that Sam did not have to sit in a cold, damp wooden shed any longer.

"How do you feel about becoming my chauffeur?" I asked him with some trepidation.

Sam looked at me and then wordlessly took the car keys from my hand. He said nothing; he just nodded his agreement.

Not for the first time, and certainly not for the last, I wondered what on earth I would do without him.

CHAPTER SIX

Out of the caravan and into the stables

'It's not easy, but it's not rocket science.'

With Sam as my chauffeur I continued to travel around the country tracking down suitable developments on behalf of investors. Friends were also a great support; in fact, it was my friend, Keith, who became instrumental in the next stage of my recovery when he introduced me to Tony Carter.

Tony was a wealthy property developer and a client of Keith's at Steggles and Mather, Solicitors. Keith introduced us not long after Tony had sold out his company, North West Estates, for a significant sum of money, using the profit to start up Norbury Developments in Marple near Stockport. Tony wanted me to work with him and proposed that we get together for an initial 12 months with me looking for suitable commercial sites and Norbury putting up the cash.

At this stage Jan and I had separated; she was living in rented accommodation in Ashton village in Cheshire with the children and I was living nearby. By now I was finding it almost impossible to pretend that our relationship was anything other than platonic and it had also become more and more obvious that we wanted different things out of life. I had not lost sight of my earlier ambitions; the 10 goals I'd wanted to achieve by the age of 30, even though I'd just passed my self imposed deadline, whereas she wanted security and stability above all else. In spite of what I had been through with LPI I was still prepared to take risks in pursuit of a better life.

Tony Carter was ambitious too and probably saw a like-minded individual in me. As he handed over the keys to a Mondeo – and I passed them on to Sam – we shook hands on our financial arrangement. I was to receive 25% on each deal I completed, effectively ensuring a regular income - as long as I tracked down the deals that suited Tony, of course.

It didn't take long for me to find the first site for Norbury Developments; an industrial estate in Droitwich. Having secured the purchase in Droitwich I then had to find a buyer and colleague Keith Williams, a property developer I'd known for some time, was the man. (Not to be confused with architect, David Williams.) We made £320k on that deal which meant my personal stake was £80k.

Fast forwarding for a moment to the present day and purely to illustrate the volatile nature of property developing, Tony Carter's company has been through tough times recently, along with so many other property developers. I helped out with a loan of £50k a year or so ago, but when it became obvious that there was no way Tony was going to be able to repay the loan, I was forced to make him bankrupt in January '09. As with LPI and more recently, David Mclean, nothing is guaranteed. We all know that the price of property doesn't have to go up; we just didn't predict how far and how fast it was going to fall.

With my personal situation now uppermost in my mind (I didn't want to live apart from the family any longer) I'd been keeping an eye on an old dilapidated stables not far from where we'd been living in Halkyn and I asked Sam to drive me over there one morning.

We both knew as we looked out of the car window at the roofless shell of a building that it needed thousands of pounds spending on it to make it habitable but I also knew it would make a perfect family home.

I tracked down the owners of the stables and managed to negotiate a good deal which meant I wouldn't have to complete on the contract and pay the full purchase price until I'd finished the renovations. Once the property was established as a family home I'd be able to either put it on the market and sell it, or raise funds for the final purchase based on the new value.

The confidence of knowing that I was going to be able to house my family again was a great boost and helped me indirectly in the deals I was continuing to negotiate for Norbury Developments. It was during one of my regular trips to London in 1997, while having lunch with colleagues in Quaglino's in Bury Street, that I was introduced to

Graham Barclay who at the time was one of the major shareholders of UK Land. Graham is also related to Sir David and Sir Frederick Barclay, the reclusive businessmen, who between them are said to be worth a total of £1.8bn. The 73-year-old twin brothers live on the private island of Brecqhou, 80 miles west of Sark in the Channel Islands, where they've built a £60m gothic-style mansion and whose extensive business empire includes the Ritz Hotel in London and the *Daily* and *Sunday Telegraph* newspapers. Although publicity-shy, the Barclay brothers have been in the news a lot recently due to their attempts to change the ancient feudal system of government on Sark where they employ almost a sixth of the residents in their various business interests. When it became clear that full democracy was not an option the brothers withdrew their support and closed down their businesses with the loss of 100 jobs.

I believed that Graham had inherited some of the twins' expertise when it came to making money; he was a classic trader and he taught me the art of funding, in other words, he told me never to use my own money when concluding a deal; always use the banks'. I was fascinated by this larger than life character; he drank more than most but he was also more charismatic than most and I didn't need much persuasion to continue our discussions at his office in Jermyn Street.

I sat down opposite him and waited for him to speak. Graham didn't beat about the bush.

"I think we could be beneficial for one another, Rob," he

said as he poured another drink. "Why don't you come and work for us at UK Land? We need someone of your calibre to run our office in Manchester."

Now, I knew that UK Land was a successful developer; at the time it was the owner of the Elephant and Castle shopping centre in south east London and I also knew that an opportunity like this didn't come along every day of the week.

"And what's the deal on offer?" I asked, knowing that it would have to be pretty good to beat the 25% that Tony was giving me at the moment.

"33%," replied Graham, which we both knew was generous. By now I was spending almost as much money as I was earning on renovating the stables in Halkyn and so a salary rise would come in very handy indeed. We shook on the deal and I told Sam the good news as we drove back up north.

"I knew things would get better soon enough," said Sam, looking at me in the rear view mirror. "Anyone who can sell marbles back to his schoolmates has got to have a good business brain. Besides, you were never cut out to be a mechanic."

I was feeling pretty invincible since shaking hands with Graham; surely I could have been a mechanic if I'd put my mind to it? I mean, it's not rocket science, is it?

"I knew when you were eight years old that you'd be better off behind a desk," continued Sam. "I once asked you to use a hammer on a jammed wheel nut and you missed and hit me on the head!"

"That explains a lot," I said, smiling.

"Well, it explains why you're better off paying contractors and not renovating Eatonfield Stables yourself, unless you're planning on Jan divorcing you some time soon. How's it going by the way?"

I wasn't sure if Sam was referring to the renovation work or the state of our marriage. It suited me to assume the former.

"Expensive," I said with a grimace and looked down again at the papers on my lap.

As soon as everything had been agreed and signed on the dotted line I got stuck into my new role at UK Land with enthusiasm.

The first big development I considered suitable was the Wellfield Shopping Centre in Bangor, North Wales and I had to travel back to London pretty soon afterwards to present my considerations to the board. I was both puzzled and concerned by their hesitation.

"We're not sure about this one," said Graham, shaking his head. "Bangor seems an awful long way away for us, Rob. We won't deny its got potential but…"

I didn't understand. Bangor might have been a distance from London, that's true, but it was perfect for my responsibilities within the company in the Northwest and I said so again.

"It's just 100 miles from Manchester," I said, prepared to explain how easy it was to travel between the two in less than a couple of hours when I suddenly realised what they were referring to.

"Are you thinking of Bangor, Northern Ireland?" I asked.

"Is there another?" queried the London-based directors.

Once I'd straightened out the misunderstanding it took me only five minutes to explain the strength of the deal. Within the hour I'd called Keith Mather in Chester and told him what was on offer. I needed him to join us immediately and travel the 200 miles to London.

"But I've got a dinner arrangement," he said.

After a bit of persuasion and reassurance from me that this was the deal to end all deals, he altered his plans, booked the next train to Euston and was in The Cumberland Hotel that evening.

Fourteen hours later UK Land (Manchester) had acquired The Wellfield Shopping Centre in Bangor North Wales from previous owners Guardian Royal Exchange and I had succeeded in concluding the fastest deal of my career; a deal that equated to a 26% net initial yield. The reason the yield was so impressive was because GRE had not taken the car park income into account.

If Graham Barclay had not been the hard-drinking, charismatic businessman that he is I doubt I would have been able to drive the deal through so quickly, as it was, the Wellfield Shopping Centre purchase became one of the high points in all my years in property development. I knew I could have sold Wellfield the next day and made £500k, instead, UK Land (Manchester) waited a year and sold it on to The Raven Group, making more than £1m. Doing the deal had been tough, but it wasn't rocket science either; it was just much, much better than being a mechanic.

I loved the thrill of the Wellfield deal because it was so quick from negotiation through to completion. In fact I think that speed is probably more important in today's difficult economic climate, which is why I've been very cautious when it comes to paying hard cash for anything I've been offered recently. As far as I'm concerned, a bird in the hand is worth two in the bush. If you're selling a development and you've got a willing buyer, why wait for a higher offer that may never come? I don't agree with marketing property to the 'nth' degree; it makes much better business sense to move on to the next deal. Of course, if market conditions mean that you can't sell quickly, it takes a very brave developer indeed to consider buying – unless, of course, you consider the offer on the table to be too good to miss.

By now Eatonfield Stables in Halkyn was almost complete and in summer 1997 Jan and I moved in to our five bedroom property with J, Jo and Dan. There were just a few final touches necessary and a bit of work still outstanding on the outbuildings but other than that it felt like a veritable palace after the cramped conditions we'd endured in the caravan. Ten year old J was overjoyed at the prospect of having a pony of his own and Jo couldn't believe that she wouldn't have to share a bedroom any longer. I was just happy to be back with my kids.

Unfortunately, there was just one blip on the horizon: I didn't have the money to pay the contractor's final invoice and he was not going to wait a moment longer for the cash I owed. That's when I first met Kevin McLeod and no, this wasn't Kevin, the avuncular presenter of TV programme, *Grand Designs,* this was a bigger, muscle-bound Kevin with a differently spelt surname and a large Alsatian dog in tow.

"Rob Lloyd?"

I looked at his imposing physique and told him that yes, I was Rob Lloyd and how could I help him.

It soon became clear that the only way I could help Kevin, or Mac as I call him, was to comply with his client's request and pay off my debt. "But I don't have the money," I said, as politely as I could.

To which he replied, without a hint of a smile, that there had to be some way for me to get it.

Mac and I ended up sharing a cup of tea in the kitchen at Eatonfield Stables and I patiently explained to him that yes, I did owe his client money but I also had bad debtors of my own. If only my creditors would pay their bills I'd have no problem settling the outstanding invoice. Mac sipped thoughtfully on his tea while trying to come up with a solution. He asked for a list of my creditors and I duly passed it over.

"If I persuade them to pay you, you'll be able to pay my client," he explained and I couldn't doubt his logic. He also made it very clear that this was my only chance; he might have appeared perfectly polite but he was certainly no pushover.

With Mac's help I was able to satisfy his client's demands and after that seemingly inauspicious start, he and I now have a very good relationship, in fact I'd go so far as to say he is probably one of my closest friends.

Following the Wellfield deal I continued to make money for UK Land (Manchester) but Graham Barclay knew that I still had an ambition to run my own business again. A couple of factors made the decision to set up Eatonfield Holdings an easy one for me: first was the fact that UK Land was considering delisting and reverting back to a private company and secondly, I had a strained relationship with Chris Woodhouse, one of the commercial directors at the company.

"Now's your chance, Rob, if you're thinking of going it alone," said Graham and using most of the equity I had made for myself over the last 18 months, that's exactly what I did next.

CHAPTER SEVEN

Success at last

'Nothing comes easy, but it's a lot to do with timing – and luck!'

In 1998 I was 34; older and wiser than I was when I'd started the LPI Group, but no less ambitious and I knew that it was the right time to go it alone again.

After the successes of UK Land (Manchester) I now had enough money behind me to take on the whole deal and not just work on commissions. The only thing I wasn't sure about was the name I was going to give my new company; I wanted it to be sufficiently different to my previous business not to conjure up painful memories, but even if it wasn't actually named after me, I wanted it to have some significance. As I turned into the drive at Eatonfield Stables I realised that a suitable name was staring me in the face, in fact I was living in it.

I started up Eatonfield Holdings in the front room with a desk and a mobile 'phone but this time the economic situation was different than it had been in 1989. The time was right, I had money to invest and I didn't waste any time investing it.

My first big deal was Canolfan Teifi, a partially vacant shopping centre in Cardigan, west Wales. The centre had gone into administration two years earlier in 1996 and had a book value of well over £1m. Eatonfield Holdings eventually acquired the four level shopping centre in August 1998 for £230k

My intention was to hold on to my investment and within 12 months I'd renovated the units and achieved a healthy level of occupancy from high street names as well as local retailers. As a by-product of the lengthy negotiations I developed a real love for this part of Wales and eventually bought a holiday cottage for the family in the area, just at the back of the high street in Cardigan.

In fact, over the next few years, we all invested a lot of time and energy in Cardigan. Eatonfield Holdings' business dealings in the area became more and more complex and expensive over the years and with frequent press coverage the residents of the town got to know us pretty well too, not all of them, I'm sorry to say, completely supportive of what we were doing. Eatonfield got really involved in the community, sponsoring the rugby club. Sam was also a frequent visitor to the town. You could say that he became a bit of a character in Cardigan.

Meanwhile, back in North Wales it was becoming obvious that I would have to move into proper offices and allow the family sole use of the house. In 2000 I scoured the area for suitable properties within a five mile radius and eventually found The Old Court House in Halkyn Street, Holywell.

This former county court building was in a pretty dilapidated state when I first saw it but it was in a very accessible position in the centre of town. It's a handsome property with some architectural significance, constructed with sandstone quoins and with attractive arched shaped windows and doors. I liked it and I knew it would be ideal, not just for Eatonfield but for other businesses who might want to share the space with us. It was on the market for £120k; I put in an offer of £40k and it was accepted.

After a quick call to my old friend and architect, David Williams, we set about transforming it into comfortable offices, eventually realising 1,943ft of space on the ground floor and 659sq ft on the first. Eatonfield moved into the rear of the ground floor with Delyn Women's Aid, a local charity, taking the front section. The rent from the charity paid the mortgage on the whole property. In 2005 when we grew too big for The Old Court House and Eatonfield had to move to larger, purpose-built offices we sold the whole building on to another property developer for £225k.

I now turned my attentions to Merseyside, the city of Liverpool in particular. This was 2001, remember, seven years before the Capital of Culture and some of my colleagues in Eatonfield where not sure that Liverpool was the market we should be investing in. In retrospect I think they may have been right.

The Rialto Centre had had a rocky and eventful past. What was once a former dance hall and cinema had been razed to the ground in 1981 during the Toxteth riots, then rebuilt in 1996 by Merseyside property firm, Rogerson's. Rogerson's had since gone into receivership and the building was now an unloved, partly let retail unit crying out for investment. Eatonfield used its expertise to rectify outstanding planning breaches relating to modifications to the car park, the railings and landscaping but it was a stressful and slow process.

In 2003 we decided to sell it on as three separate sites. The nine retail units in the Rialto Shopping Centre were now fully let but it had been a difficult development. On balance, even though we paid £300k and doubled our money in two years, I felt it best in future to stick with the areas we knew and one of the areas I knew best was North Wales.

Peblig Mill Industrial Estate was one of Eatonfield's most ambitious purchases. In 2002 we bought this 28 acre site on the outskirts of Caernarfon for £360k from Wardle Storeys of Essex and invested in the refurbishment of the units with the intention of boosting the rental income with new tenants.

The site consisted of 19 acres of development land off the A4085 Beddgelert to Caernarfon road and a further nine acre undeveloped site on the opposite side of the road. There was also 250,000sq ft of usable buildings, most of which had lain empty for years. We wanted to refresh the

Me with Sam

With Uncle Frank Banner

Me and Sam, ready to get stuck in

*Me on my tractor and
Sam on his*

Uncle Bill Roberts

Bill Roberts with the 1958 Grand National entry on Princess Garter

Me with cousins Paula & Andrew

Competing on Junior, clearing the last jump

In the stable yard at Lodge Farm

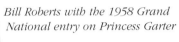

Me and Sam, another busy day!

With Crispin

*At the Cheshire
Forest Hunt*

Mum and Dad

*Me and Grandma,
Margaret Alice Lloyd*

With the Rydal tennis team, front row 1st left

*English 'O'level pass, 'if at
first you don't succeed....'*

*The Rydal Colts XV, front row
2nd from the right*

In my LPI days, a sponsored run for the Dodleston Foundation with the residents of the village cheering us on

Running the car park in Albion Street

The Jag....

J on Waterstown Sally in the Junior Hicksted Derby

Jo, J and Dan at the caravan

Dan sitting proudly on Sherry

Jo, Sam, Dan & J with Scooby Doo and Robin at Clifton

Handing over the Dodleston Foundation cheque to the Duke of Westminster

Left-Right, David McLean, Peter Stevenson, Simon Rodenhurst, me and far right, Simon Carter at the Levitt Golf Tournament

whole area, bringing in much needed jobs and held extensive talks with Gwynedd County Council about maximising the site's potential. We were also in discussion with the Welsh Development Agency.

David Williams took responsibility for the design of the units; Matthew Neeley was our construction manager and Steve Hopwood led most of the day to day renovations. The sheer volume of work often meant that Steve and his team had to work until the early hours of the morning in preparation for an incoming tenant but we always managed to pull it off because as I mentioned earlier, I now realised the importance of surrounding myself with good people. David, Matthew and Steve were three of the best; in fact, Steve still works for me at Rob Lloyd Racing and is one of my most trusted employees.

Within two years the annual rental income at Peblig Mill rose from £36k to more than £300k and in March 2004 we sold for £2m, with the adjoining land adding a further £135k in April 2005.

By 2002 Eatonfield was valued at £5m, not bad for a company I'd started just four years earlier as Eatonfield Holdings. We'd since added Eatonfield Facilities Management, our contracting and shop fitting division; Eatonfield Asset Management which kept an eye on our longer term assets and Eatonfield Special Projects which looked after the management of various development opportunities.

The local press in North Wales was now following us

with interest and I gave an interview in June 2002 to the *Daily Post* which discussed our philosophy in a bit more detail. I explained that part of our success was down to us ensuring that the sites we chose for development were given a better identity once they came within our control thanks to quality refurbishment and long term vision. I also explained that we were buying a lot of receivership quality stock so we were able to offer discounts, very competitive rents and flexible lease terms to tenants. We also believed it was important not to be too greedy and always enhance value. Peblig was a good example of this philosophy.

The years 1998 to 2005 were also productive ones for us in west Wales. Eatonfield Holdings was heavily involved in the Cardigan Regeneration Plan where we worked closely with Ceredigion County Council and the Welsh Development Agency discussing town centre regeneration as well as out of town developments. The development sites and plans for the scheme included a 70,000sq ft shopping mall with residential accommodation and additional parking facilities, as well as a 12 acre site for a supermarket.

But even though the years in Cardigan were productive, they were not productive enough. We spent hundreds of thousands of pounds on professional advice but still the Welsh Development Agency's grants were not forthcoming and there was strong opposition from a few local people and councillors.

Headlines in the local newspaper *Tivy-Side* probably said

it all: *'Shock, welcome and caution'*. Those three words perfectly encapsulated the ambiguous attitude of some residents in Cardigan at what we were trying to do. There was *shock* at the design that architects John Taylor Associates had come up with for the shopping centre in town which some considered to be too modern, there was *welcome* for the substantial long-term economic boost but *caution* at the proposed supermarket site at the northern end of town. Eatonfield's plans were all part of a much needed £12m regeneration of Cardigan but opposition to change of any sort was pretty vociferous from some quarters.

We printed a brochure for distribution outlining our vision for Cardigan. We explained how we believed our plans would improve the economy and bring much needed jobs to the area. We detailed our intention to buy and develop the Clynderwen and Cardiganshire Farmers Ltd building in the centre of town and to develop the two thirds of an acre site around it and we expressed our firm belief that developing Cardigan as a whole was the right thing to do in order to bring sustained prosperity to the area.

By now we had agreed to pre-let 60% of the proposed new retail units in the centre of town but still we faced opposition. Planning was proving protracted and extremely complicated with councillors divided in their opinion. There were some who almost accused us of blackmail; saying that if Eatonfield didn't get permission for the out-of-town supermarket we were threatening not to invest in the regeneration scheme at all. Nothing could have been further from the truth; it was just that without a grant from the WDA for the town centre development there would be a huge shortfall in available cash and a commitment from a food retailer would have bridged that gap. We needed planning for the out of town development to make the whole project a viable one.

On a lighter note, the years spent battling the planners in Cardigan meant that I got to spend a lot of time in a beautiful part of the country. We had some fantastic family holidays at the cottage but even that couldn't ease the frustration. Most people know me as the man who doesn't give up but when Eatonfield Holdings was approached by Modus Properties I knew I had to consider selling. There is a limit to how much a relatively small developer like Eatonfield can spend without a return and the disappointment that we had still not received a grant from the WDA was a bone of contention for me. I also felt there was a certain group of people who didn't want this to happen in Cardigan – no matter what – and so I spoke to Brendan Flood, MD of Modus about a possible sale.

Manchester-based Modus is the third largest shopping centre developer in the country and has the ability to invest on a larger scale than Eatonfield so in November 2005 we sold most of the sites and plans in Cardigan to Modus for £6.275m and Eatonfield was left with just a few small properties in the centre of town.

Visiting Cardigan today, not much has changed. Modus also struggled with planning issues as well as opposition from residents and has now sold on a substantial amount of its investment too.

I was disappointed that others didn't share Eatonfield's belief that investing in a modern retail development was the right thing to do for Cardigan and it puzzles me that a vociferous minority can win the day, because that was what it was; a minority. There was a significant amount of local support for our plans but one or two who viewed Eatonfield as a threat and in the end we didn't have the resources to continue fighting. I learnt to take that realisation in my stride, but it wasn't easy because I had become so personally attached to the area. As a family we had grown to love Cardigan; in fact we lived and breathed the area, particularly Sam. That's why in 2008, when Sam died, I couldn't forgive those he knew in the town for failing to come to his funeral; not one of the friends he made in the area over the last seven years made the three hour trip to Wrexham to pay their respects. And that fact, more than the failure to secure a future in Cardigan for Eatonfield, left me feeling very disappointed indeed.

And yet I never truly gave up on Cardigan. The year Sam died an opportunity presented itself for Eatonfield to get involved again and I grabbed it with both hands. In 2008 we agreed to buy back a significant chunk of the development from Modus.

Meanwhile, concurrent developments were keeping us

busy. We bought and sold 50,000sq ft of industrial units at the Bryn Lane Complex near Wrexham; we bought two sites on Eastfield Industrial Estate, three miles from Scarborough making a profit of £1m; and we bought the 2.3 acre Post Office distribution centre in Driffield in east Yorkshire where we put in a planning application to knock down existing buildings with the intention of marketing the whole site with Liverpool based developer, Ethel Austin Properties. At the end of 2008 we exchanged contracts to sell.

When deciding which sites to invest in, Eatonfield's business model is pretty straightforward; each development prospect has to fit within a balanced portfolio against an agreed set of priorities to ensure it achieves at least the planned rate of return. For commercial property that means a target rate of return of 25%. The potential profit from a development is always considered on a 'best, worst and most likely' basis, which means looking at the short term exit strategy as well as the ultimate opportunity.

We've become very good at adding value to the properties in our portfolio since we revalue for an estimated return at each stage of the development. This also means we can draw down and leverage further loans. Confidence in our ability also comes with knowing the type of buyer likely to step in when we decide to sell. The extensive network of contacts we've built up over the years is invaluable in this respect.

Eatonfield was going from strength to strength. Following

on from our many successes in commercial property developing we were about to raise the bar once more and turn our attention to residential property. However, just in case anyone should think my life was plain sailing through the years of growth, the reality couldn't have been further from the truth. Professionally, things were progressing smoothly for us, that's true, but on a personal level my life was much more complicated.

CHAPTER EIGHT

Who wants to be a millionaire?

'Property and horses are in Dad's blood, the family is in his heart, but who can guess what's in his head!'

In 1999, twelve months after setting up Eatonfield, I knew that my new company was built on much firmer foundations than LPI. I said in an interview with local newspaper, the *Daily Post,* that I wanted us to treble our asset base in the next two to three years. I also stated with complete confidence that one of the important points to bear in mind on the route to successful property developing was to know when to say 'no'; in other words of the 20 developments Eatonfield could be offered at any one time there might only be two that are suitable for us and the skill comes in recognising which two they are. I've always said that the next deal is important; the key is choosing which deal that should be. Unfortunately, when it came to my personal life I was much less confident.

My wife and I were sharing our home at Eatonfield Stables but we weren't sharing anything else in our lives.

There was no animosity in our relationship; it's just that we were living more like brother and sister than husband and wife. I stayed at Eatonfield Stables because I'd made a promise to myself that I wouldn't leave the marriage until the children were older and in 2000 J was 13, Jo was 11 and Dan was nine. The two eldest were now boarding at Rydal, but Dan was still at primary school. My family is extremely important to me and I didn't want to jeopardise their happiness if I could help it.

All three children are keen riders and my old pal Keith Shore had given them lessons right from the start. J went on to ride for Wales and competed at the Junior British Jumping Derby at Hickstead in 1999. At one point we had 13 ponies at Eatonfield, all ridden by the children and occasionally by me but in 2000 I injured myself quite badly and have struggled to get back in the saddle ever since.

I slipped a disc lifting the tailgate on one of the horseboxes, even though I knew that this was something you should only ever do with two people. As usual I was in a rush and hoisted it up myself.

I didn't realise how serious it was at first and assumed it was a bad strain that would eventually heal itself but, of course, it didn't. The pain got worse and worse until I could barely walk. In the end I had to go to hospital where I ended up having an epidural but nothing seemed to ease the discomfort and the doctor eventually advised remedial massage. I'm sure his advice was well meant but I barely had time to go to the surgery for a five minute appointment, let alone half an hour with a masseur. Nevertheless, when I spotted a leaflet advertising 'remedial massage for back injuries' I picked it up and stuffed it in my pocket, but picking up the 'phone and making an appointment took me at least another week.

Helen Wilson was a beauty therapist and masseur, who at the time was based in Stockton Heath near Warrington. Her salon was convenient for the motorway so I called to make an appointment, which I then subsequently went on to cancel. I also cancelled the next three appointments after that, thanks to the pressure of work, so by the time I actually walked into 'The Green Room' in 2001 I'm pretty sure Helen thought I was a fantasist who got his kicks from making appointments for massages he had no intention of keeping.

"Aaah, Mr Lloyd, I presume?" she said with a wry smile, once I finally walked in and sheepishly introduced myself.

If I could just say one thing in my defence: at least Helen knew what she was taking on when she met me. For better or worse, I am exactly the same man today as the one she met seven years ago; I'm always busy and I'm always running late. I also very quickly applied the same principle to Helen as I do to all the other important people in my life; I shortened her name and started to call her 'H'.

But there was one part of me that did change on that day in 2001; I walked into the salon a stressed out businessman and walked out someone who now realised that there was more to life than work. After my first massage I made other appointments for The Green Room - and turned up for every one of them.

Over the next couple of months H and I built up a special rapport and it wasn't just the massages I found beneficial. I would lie on the table and, as she worked hard at getting rid of my back pain, I would tell her all the things about my life that I'd never discussed with anyone before. There were plenty of people I could talk to about business; my colleagues at Eatonfield and contacts in the wider property world would join me in a discussion on the potential profit on a deal at the drop of a hat, but I had no-one to talk to about the personal side of my life.

The time I spent with H gradually became the most important part of my whole week. I knew what I wanted and it was Helen, although in the beginning I couldn't honestly say that she felt the same way about me. It was six weeks or so before she let me get up off the massage table to talk to her over dinner and not before I'd presented her with expensive chocolates and bottles of champagne. I suppose I courted her in an old-fashioned, romantic way, but I knew I'd get there eventually.

"You're very confident, aren't you?" she said, in an accusing manner.

"Well, I'm certainly confident of one thing," I replied.

"And what's that?"

"I'm confident that you are my ideal woman and because of that I'm prepared to wait – for as long as it takes."

I remember kissing her that night and it felt as if I'd never kissed anyone else in my life before that moment.

H and I started meeting as regularly as we could. She found it more difficult than I did as she often had clients in the evening but for once I was prepared to wait. At this stage we were both in pretty deep; we knew we were falling in love and the guilt we both felt because of that was almost unbearable. H and her husband had no children of their own but she seemed to understand how important mine were to me almost straight away.

"You're very lucky," she said when I told her about J, Jo and Dan and I couldn't help thinking that if my children met Helen they would almost certainly hit it off, but much as I wanted to, I knew I couldn't let that happen.

We were communicating on the 'phone now two or three times a day and at some point during our two year affair Jan found out. She confronted me and I panicked. I knew H and I would have to stop seeing each other because I was haunted by the thought of losing the kids and I arranged to meet H in a pub in Stockton Heath to tell her that we couldn't go on like this any longer.

I tried to finish it and I think I said all the right words but all I can remember is feeling absolutely distraught when I got back to the car.

By the time I pulled up at Eatonfield Stables I was completely numb. Jan looked at me and could tell that something serious had happened and I've never forgotten what she said:

"You'll never finish with Helen; you just can't keep away

from her."

Two days later I called H and she agreed to see me. I was so relieved; I'd been petrified that she would never forgive me for what I'd done, but she did and I knew then that she loved me as much as I loved her.

All I could think of now was introducing H to J, Jo and Dan but I had to give some serious thought to the idea of getting divorced first. I wanted to put our relationship on a firmer footing; I knew as clearly as I'd ever known anything in my life that H was 'The One'; she was the woman of my dreams, the woman who had first appeared on my list of 10 goals in life 18 years before but whom I'd only just met.

That summer Jan announced she was going on holiday without the children, taking her mother on a coach trip to Italy. She got chatting to the coach driver, Dave, and realised that they had a lot in common.

Dave has a few attributes I don't share; chief among them the fact he has a steady job and he's unlikely to announce that he wants to own a racing stables in the future, which suited Jan down to the ground. We decided it was time to end our marriage.

In 2002 we obtained a quickie divorce on the understanding that I take the blame for the break up of the marriage and agree to be cited as the guilty party. I wasn't happy with this at all but it was the price I had to pay to keep Eatonfield Stables and for H and I to be together.

Now that everything was out in the open and just before the divorce was finalised I decided it was time for H and the children to meet.

I arranged to take J, Jo and Dan to The Green Room, with the idea, I suppose, that it was neutral ground and therefore less stressful for everyone concerned. Helen, however, was a bag of nerves.

"You're bringing them here? To the salon? What are we going to talk about?"

"I don't know. Perhaps you could do Jo's nails?" I suggested helpfully. And that's exactly what H did, or should I say; tried to do. Her hands were shaking so much she only just managed it.

After meeting at the salon we all went for a Chinese meal and any nervousness I'd felt at the prospect of my three children meeting Helen had now completely disappeared. H and Jo were to become particularly close over the years and the boys also welcomed her into our family without a moment's hesitation. I was a very lucky man.

I knew I was going to have to sell our cottage in Cardigan to finance the divorce so I suggested that the five of us go to west Wales for the weekend before it was sold. The girls were going to be sharing a bedroom so I braced myself for fallout from their conversations. Would they like each other? What would Jo say about me as a dad? Would H welcome the idea of being a step-mum?

Apparently Jo informed H that I had 'blond' moments at home which didn't quite fit my image of the organised, dynamic businessman I'd created for myself. She also told her that family, work and horses were important to me - in that order. J put it slightly more poetically: "Property and horses are in Dad's blood, the family is in his heart, but who can guess what's in his head!"

H and I began our life at Eatonfield Stables in Halkyn in the autumn of 2002, but within 12 months it was obvious that H felt uncomfortable living in a property that had been built for my first wife.

"Wouldn't you like more space?" she asked, which I had to admit, I hadn't thought about recently. I was hoping we might need a bigger house in the future, once we had children of our own but Jo and Dan were both at Rydal and J had just started two years of sixth form at Gordonstoun in Scotland, so Eatonfield Stables seemed big enough at the moment.

Sadly, over the next couple of years it became clear that H and I were not able to increase the size of our family. A course of IVF was unsuccessful and in the end we decided to concentrate on the three children we already had rather than try for any more.

But the idea of a bigger house still sounded like an attractive proposition. I was very interested in the idea of an extra room to accommodate a snooker table (of course) and a gym would be handy too. So we put Eatonfield Stables on the market and began looking for another property in the area.

It wasn't long before we discovered Fron Farm, a collection of derelict farm buildings with 17 acres, a mile or so from Eatonfield Stables and over the next couple of years we spent a lot of time and energy making it into a spacious family home – complete with snooker room.

We sold Eatonfield Stables at the end of 2003 for just under £500k. Four years later, the family living in the property at that time needed to sell quickly and contacted me to ask if I was interested in buying it back. I offered £250k but they turned me down. Given the state of the property market in 2009 I wonder if my offer would be considered a good one if I made it today?

As my personal life settled down, my business life also continued to improve. In 2003 I stated in an interview with the *Daily Post* that Eatonfield was interested in developing Everton Football Club's dream home. At the time of the interview Eatonfield was one of four firms in negotiations with the Merseyside club and I was more than hopeful of my plans to bankroll the new waterfront stadium and club.

I am, in fact, a lifelong Liverpool supporter, but that had no bearing on my attempts to negotiate a good deal; this was business after all. Everton wanted to raise £30m from the sale of its freehold properties, including Goodison Park, in order to finance its share of the 55,000 all-seater stadium at Kings Dock. I told the journalist interviewing me in January 2003 that Eatonfield was totally sincere in its intentions; we weren't in the habit of spending this amount of time, with all the professional back up that entailed, on a no-hope situation, but I also made it clear that any deal would be subject to planning permission being granted to allow Eatonfield to develop the other sites in the way it wanted. The other three developers had the same conditions attached to their proposals too, of course.

I visited Everton's Deputy Chairman, Bill Kenwright, twice in London to discuss the deal. I also had meetings with supermarket giant, Tesco, to talk about the possibility of bringing them on site too.

Once again, as with the Rialto Centre, Liverpool proved to be a difficult market for Eatonfield and this time no deal ensued. My £30m pledge to help Everton get their dream home eventually died a death and in 2009 Everton Football Club's ground remains Goodison Park.

On a more positive note, Eatonfield was awarded a certificate for fast growth in 2003, recognised as one of the fastest growing businesses in Wales but the downside to this was that with all the pressure of work it became very difficult for H and I to spend any quality time together. If I wasn't at The Old Court House in Holywell, I was travelling round the country attending meetings or looking for new possibilities for Eatonfield.

Even today if H and I are meeting friends for dinner I'll often turn up 10 minutes before we're due to go out and she'll have to find out about my day by listening to the conversation I'm having with the other guests around the table.

And so I promised H that I was going to try to relax a little more, but she and I both know that due to my workload I can't take a big chunk of holiday at any one time. There's also no getting away from the fact that I find it impossible to sit still; I enjoy being busy and I enjoy work. As a result, H has become particularly good at planning short, memorable breaks, none more so than the fabulous weekend she planned for my 40th birthday in 2004.

But before I describe the weekend to end all weekends I'd just like to reflect on my ten goals in life and say that this was the year that I was officially declared a millionaire – on paper. There was no great fanfare when I realised it, just a sense of achievement that I'd now reached another one of the goals that I'd set out for myself 21 years before.

And I was just about to realise another dream: owning a house with a long drive and a snooker room. H and I had taken two years to renovate the old farmhouse at Fron Farm and I began to think about starting another business, one I had been considering for a while. As J had so aptly put it: 'Property and horses' were in my blood and Fron Farm, with its 17 acres of land and private, secluded spot overlooking the Dee Estuary was perfect for the new business I had in mind: bloodstock breeding.

Meanwhile, H was taking care of the 'staying in the best hotels' category on my list. I hadn't bought the Bentley yet; I didn't own a racing yard and I hadn't got close to training a Grand National winner, but at least I was starting to find time for charity work, albeit on a small scale. I was happy with my achievements so far, but I was still aiming for all 10 goals before too long.

CHAPTER NINE

Building in the Bahamas

'"You know, don't you Rob, that you have to treat me like a thoroughbred or you may end up married to a nag?".'

"Where are we going?" I asked. It was the morning of 16th January 2004 and it was my 40th birthday.

"Skibo Castle," replied Helen. "It's in Scotland. Happy Birthday, Rob."

I pictured a draughty, cold ruin on the top of a hill and grimaced; it wasn't my idea of a luxurious weekend away, that's for sure.

Fortunately, my image of Skibo Castle couldn't have been further from reality. Skibo Castle is actually a magnificent turreted hotel set in 7,000 acres of spectacular grounds. It was built in the early 20th century as a private home for American steel magnate and philanthropist, Andrew Carnegie but was bought by the property developer Peter De Savary in 1990. Since then it has been sold on to an anonymous syndicate of members and has been refurbished to a very high standard. It has a glamorous spa and Edwardian swimming pool, both perfect for H, ancient fireplaces, huge claw-footed baths and four-poster beds. Sports facilities include an 18-hole links golf course, salmon and trout fishing, clay-pigeon shooting, tennis, badminton, rowing, canoeing, bird-watching, off-road driving, snooker, archery, croquet, target shooting, mountain biking - and a stables. Even I can't get bored here. There are also some quirky, unique touches such as communal dining for all the guests and a kilted piper to greet you on the terrace each morning.

Many of the huge rooms in the castle are lined with the original oak panelling and have massive floor to ceiling windows, thick padded curtains and ornate light fittings hanging from every ceiling. The overall impression is very grand but also very comfortable.

Most people will have heard of Skibo Castle after Madonna and Guy Ritchie chose it as the venue for their wedding in December 2000. When we were visiting, most of the guests were businessmen or professionals; experts in their field such as the eminent lawyer from Philadelphia who entertained us with some fascinating legal tales and the Russian billionaire, Boris Berezovsky. Boris sat down next to me one evening at dinner and I couldn't resist a chat, man to man, while his bodyguard kept watch by the door. We talked about politics, his love of London and the importance of using a helicopter to get to Skibo but, as far as I can remember, bearing in mind we'd all enjoyed a fair amount of wine that night, he didn't give me any tips on how to become a billionaire.

H could tell that I'd enjoyed the weekend and I'd love nothing more than to make a return visit, but we'd have to join the private members club at Skibo, known as the Carnegie Club, in order to do that. Membership costs about £7,500 a year which would mean we'd then have unlimited opportunities to enjoy this peaceful, romantic setting as often as we wanted. Unfortunately it would also mean I would have to commit to make the journey north at least a couple of times a year to make it worth our while and frankly, I'm not sure I can do that. Life is just too hectic at the moment and the added stress of not being able to get away would just defeat the point.

But H did manage to persuade me to take another break the following year; this time to Ragdale Hall in Leicestershire but nothing could live up to Skibo in my opinion. H spoiled me for my 40th birthday and the memory will always remain a high spot.

Once we got back home to Fron Farm I knew I had to give more thought to the idea of spending more time with H and decided that one solution would be for H to learn to ride. If I could find a reliable, trustworthy and patient horse then I'd even be tempted to get back in the saddle myself. We had the facilities at Fron Farm; a manège and plenty of stables, so there was no reason why it couldn't be done.

"Will you teach me?" H asked a little tentatively.

"Of course."

"Do you promise?"

"I promise," I said and meant it. I knew it wouldn't be a problem for me to teach H to ride but when it came to the finer things in life, she had taught me more than I could ever teach her and I thought I ought to show my appreciation.

"Ah, yes," she said, "And maybe now I can start teaching you about the needs and wants of a woman." I looked at her, not sure what was coming next. "How many women do you know, Rob, who would be happy with the fact that the lounge in their home is a work in progress, while the snooker room is almost finished?"

It was true; I had been directing the builders' time and efforts to my first priority – the snooker room - rather than anywhere else in the house. "You've got a point," I admitted. "Perhaps I have been a bit too...focused."

"You know, don't you Rob, that you have to treat me like a thoroughbred or you may end up married to a nag?"

I knew H was joking, but she'd made me think. I'm single-minded about most things in my life; it doesn't matter what it is. I concentrate completely on what I'm doing to the exclusion of everything else, which can be very frustrating for anyone else caught up in the maelstrom, particularly if they don't share my enthusiasm. Poor H was not a snooker fan.

But the upside of this is that it gets you noticed. This was the period in my professional life, 2003 to 2006, when I was very involved in finding and developing sites in Cardigan and, if you recall, occasionally coming up against vocal opposition.

In 2004 the local newspaper, *Tivy-Side,* was reviewing what Eatonfield had been up to in the area in the last 12 months and concluded that we were a name to watch. They also stated that my commitment to Cardigan had been *'vibrantly kept to the fore'* and went on to label me as a *'business sharp shooter.'* Sometimes then, it pays to be single minded.

For the year ended March 2004 Eatonfield's turnover was more than £3m with a gross profit of £880k. We were doing well and I wanted to expand. I'd come up with a way to include H's expertise as a qualified beautician in Eatonfield's future and in 2004 Eatonfield Leisure was born.

But first, I thought it was about time that I made our relationship official and so I asked H to marry me. Fortunately she didn't make me wait too long before saying yes and on Sunday 1st August 2004 we got married in a beautiful ceremony at Soughton Hall in North Wales with J and Dan as my best men.

I felt as if life couldn't get any better; I had the woman of my dreams, three children that any man would be proud of and a business that was making a very healthy profit.

Helen's influence didn't take long to make an impression on me. Prior to meeting her I didn't know what Gucci was, let alone consider wearing it but she introduced a bit of style into my life, starting with my wardrobe and continuing with The Ocean Club on Paradise Island where we went for our honeymoon. Fortunately I didn't know anything about the crisis just around the corner that was about to blight my personal and professional life, and all because we chose to holiday in the Bahamas.

We flew Virgin Upper Class to Nassau which was the perfect way to begin our seven days in paradise. I've always been a big fan of Richard Branson's and flying on one of his 'planes was a real personal thrill.

Not long after touching down at the airport, H and I were standing with our bags outside the terminal, waiting for transport to take us to our hotel, when we saw a shiny white limo pull up. We watched, fascinated, as Gordon Ramsay, the celebrity chef, strode purposefully over to greet the driver, bending down to say a few words through the open window.

"Rob Lloyd?" asked the chauffeur, looking over Gordon's shoulder at H and me and, looking startled at first, we nodded, as a rather large smile spread across my face. I can't remember if Gordon swore at any stage in the proceedings, but I do remember feeling that our accommodation would have to be pretty good to top my experience of the Bahamas so far.

And it was. The One & Only Club on Paradise Island was everything I imagined and more. In fact, our resort became the location for several scenes in 2006's remake of the film Casino Royale and if it's good enough for Daniel Craig, then it's good enough for me.

Our honeymoon suite came with 24 hour butler service,

the most luxurious bathroom I'd ever come across and the best sports facilities money could buy. Since my back injury I'd become a big fan of tennis and during our week's stay I played almost every day.

"This is wonderful," said H one evening as we were getting ready to go out for dinner. She was lying in the bath, surrounded by bubbles, sipping a cup of tea. I loved the fact she was enjoying a down-to-earth cuppa surrounded by all this five-star luxury and I agreed with her; it was all pretty wonderful. For the first time in my life I was relaxing on holiday and not constantly working while I was there. Although I'd loved visiting our cottage in Cardigan I tended to spend half the time immersed in details of my latest property deal. At the One & Only Club I wasn't doing that; at least not yet. The truth was I was bowled over by the Bahamas and I had been hatching a plan in the last day or two. "What do you think about us buying a place here?" I asked H.

"What?" She sat up and almost knocked her cup of tea into the water.

"Well, I had to sell our cottage in Wales to pay for the divorce; what about substituting it with a mansion here on Paradise Island?"

"You're kidding?" said Helen, although I could tell she was hoping I wasn't.

"No – and I've already done some research. I met a guy at the tennis club called Jan Ward; he's a local attorney with a lot of contacts. He says he could help us to build the mansion of our dreams on Paradise Island. I've mentioned a few requirements to Ward already: sea view, seven bedrooms, veranda – everything we could want. It'd be fantastic."

"It would," she said, then almost as an afterthought, added: "But how much would it cost?"

"About $800k," I said, having already done the sums.

"Can we afford to do it?"

"It might be a case of can we afford not to do it," I replied with a smile. H looked at me as if all the sun, sea and sand had affected my brain until I saw realisation dawn on her face. I suppose the problem was, you could take the man out of the world of property developing but you couldn't take the world of property developing out of the man, not even when he's on his honeymoon.

"What is it this time?" she asked with interest.

I sat closer to her on the edge of the bath. "Ward and I have been discussing the opportunities for building affordable homes for the Bahamians. With my experience and his contacts it would be perfect. The plan is; I'll make arrangements for a return trip, probably in September, when he is going to introduce me to Shane Gibson, the government housing minister. There's a desperate need for properties at around the $80k level and I'm pretty sure Eatonfield could be the developer to provide them."

"But you don't build houses, Rob. You invest in commercial developments."

"Yes, but I know plenty of house builders who would be

interested in coming in with us. I'll be putting the deal together." And as plenty of people had told me in the past; putting a deal together was what I was good at.

I said goodbye to Jan Ward before H and I took our Virgin flight back to the UK. We exchanged business cards. "I'll be in touch," I said, shaking his hand. "I'll see you back on Paradise Island in September."

As H and I boarded our 'plane at Nassau airport I was on a high; the plan to build affordable homes in the Bahamas was a good one and I believed that Jan Ward was a very good contact. Nothing could go wrong.

Once we got back to the UK and with memories of our honeymoon still fresh in my mind, I spent a lot of time thinking about the plans I had in the Bahamas for Eatonfield and for us personally. As I'd mentioned to H, there were two things I wanted to do; firstly, build our own mansion on Paradise Island and secondly, establish a company, under the Eatonfield banner, to construct affordable homes for local buyers.

I visited Paradise Island again in September of that year and came back even more convinced that both ideas were good ones. However, I didn't want to rush into any decisions without satisfying myself that I'd gone over every detail with Jan Ward first and with that in mind he and I spent many long distance 'phone calls during the rest of 2004 and early 2005 discussing the deal.

In the meantime I decided to concentrate on Eatonfield Leisure, H's new business venture.

CHAPTER TEN

Awards all round

'I'd much rather just get on with the next deal than have a panel of 'experts' telling me how well I've done on the last one.'

H and I found the perfect location for Eatonfield Leisure at Stretton, near Warrington, within a half an hour's drive of some of the most moneyed areas of Cheshire including Knutsford, Wilmslow and Alderley Edge. We couldn't wait to get started on the conversion of the two dilapidated farm buildings and put in the necessary planning permissions for the transformation. Most of the neighbours in the area were happy to have the old eyesore transformed - everyone that is except Mr Emmis.

There was a party wall between the spa and Emmis' property. He refused to let us go on his land to do the necessary pointing on the brickwork and called the police several times to complain. Then one day he lost it completely and came at me with a stick, threatening to do 'some serious damage' if I didn't clear off.

Now, I'm not a violent man but if there's one thing I can't stand it's a bully. As soon as I saw the stick I grabbed hold of the ladder, climbed over the fence and started to do the repair work myself with Steve Hopwood not far behind. I was not going to be threatened by anyone, least of all someone who would rather live next door to a rat infested barn than a luxurious £500k spa. Eatonfield Leisure had cost more money in planning than it should have done, thanks to Emmis and I was not going to be sidetracked a moment longer.

In the world of property developing you are always going to come up against difficulties and I don't just mean the legitimate planning problems that are part and parcel of everyday life, I mean the awkward neighbours like Emmis, the clients who can't pay their bills or, worse still, the clients who can pay their bills but won't. That's when it's a good idea to have a friend like Mac. He's told me stories of bad debtors held out of windows by their ankles until invoices have been paid, and I thanked my lucky stars that I'd paid Mac's client when he'd asked. Fortunately nothing like that was necessary here and on June 29th The Eatonfield Day Spa was officially opened by the Coronation Street actress, Beverley Callard.

Before long, H was being nominated for awards for her business skills. She won the 'Women in Business' category at Trinity Mirror Business Awards in 2005, accepting her award at a gala dinner in October that year. The judges said they were looking for innovation, management skills and achievement and H made a short speech saying she was thrilled with her success. I was very proud of her.

Unfortunately, my pride and H's experience couldn't make the spa pay. Eatonfield Day Spa was a very staff-intensive business with high overheads and small margins. H had built up a client database of 2,000 from absolutely nothing but it had been a stressful process and in October 2006 we sold out for £825k. It had been an interesting and exciting journey but the bottom line was; we weren't making a profit. Eatonfield Leisure is no longer a going concern and H has since moved on to establish her own online antiques business.

In 2004 Eatonfield had a business development team including Land Director Jonathan Richards. We had strong relationships with house builders, retailers and banks and as a result we were being offered more and more developments. We also became expert at adding value to the properties in our portfolio. We would evaluate the implications of outstanding local authority conditions on the development proposals, complete surveys highlighting challenges and opportunities and we would also assess the possible change of use. We would then revalue at each stage of the development to negotiate further loans or simply to determine the overall return on the portfolio. We then made sure we had a regular review of progress against budgeted turnover.

In 2005 in the period to the end of June, Eatonfield's turnover had increased to £4.7m, leaping to £17m by June

2006. Running my own business this time round was very different to the late 80s and early 90s which had been so difficult for LPI. The market was in our favour now and I had learnt from past mistakes. I listened to advice and realised the importance of having other good people around me; people like Legal Director, Keith Mather, Accounts Controller, Phil Middlehurst, Development Director, Ian Arnott, and Planning Director, Steve Jones; all invaluable members of the team.

I also knew that a lot of Eatonfield's success was down to finding the right financial package for the deal we were doing at the time and, as our brand was going from strength to strength, it made sense to offer that expertise to others. In December 2005 we launched Eatonfield Business Solutions.

Meanwhile, H was determined we should start enjoying life together, and I agreed, just as soon as I got my bloodstock business off the ground.

Cloverdale Bloodstock started life at Fron Farm in 2005. It's a fairly straightforward business in that we keep mares and foals but no stallions, sending the mares away to be covered. Once the foals are yearlings a large number of them will be sold at Doncaster or Tattersalls sales, but in the next few years we hope that some of the foals will be bought by outside owners who will put them with Rob Lloyd Racing for training.

Cloverdale was my way of bringing horses back into my life in some way. I couldn't afford to open a racing stables at this stage and as far as I was concerned this was the next best thing. Once that had been achieved, I promised H I would try to find more time for the family.

In 2005 the Bahamas also loomed large in our lives. I had been back to the island in July meeting both Jan Ward and his brother Monty, who was a close colleague of the Bahamian Housing Minister, Shane Gibson. Gibson confirmed at our meeting that the supply of affordable homes for islanders was extremely limited, indicating to us that as many as 7,000 houses needed to be built to satisfy demand.

In September of that year I went back to the Bahamas once again, this time with Keith Mather, Eatonfield's Legal Director. Our meetings with Shane Gibson and Jan Ward progressed well and following Ward's information that a number of deposits had already been received from prospective buyers, Keith set up the joint venture agreement. We were reliably informed that the waiting list for our new, low cost, $80k homes was now standing at 14,000. We didn't actually see evidence of the waiting list and we didn't see details of bank deposits, but at this stage we had no reason to doubt the information we were being given.

However, one or two alarm bells did ring when Ward offered me what can only be described as a 'three in a bed' opportunity.

I was in the car with Ward and his female colleague, driving back to Nassau, when he asked me if I would like to 'relax' together. I wasn't sure I knew what Ward was getting at but I guessed 'together' meant a three in a bed romp.

"Together?" I queried and he nodded and smiled, obviously pleased I'd got the message straight away. I couldn't get out of the car fast enough.

"I think you'd better drop me off at my hotel," I said, opening the door before we'd even come to a halt.

Ward said no more on the matter but it was fairly obvious to me that this was not the first time he'd had set up this sort of 'meeting' and I wondered how many other business associates had fallen for it. Perhaps it was ammunition for Ward if a deal ever went sour on him?

In November 2005, H and I went back to Paradise Island with Keith and his wife Min for the grand opening of the office. As we walked through the terminal building and out into the sunlight a 20ft bright yellow banner was there to greet us stating:

'Own your own dream home. The easy way. Come in and talk to one of our advisers.'

There was a 'phone number and a logo, alongside our name: 'Eatonfield Construction'.

All four of us paused for a moment.

"Dave's done a great job," I said, referring to Dave Lloyd of Wise Monkey Design, a local firm we use for much of our design and marketing work. "Who wouldn't want to buy their dream home here on Nassau after seeing that?"

Dave had also produced posters, leaflets and information

booklets for any local Bahamian wishing to invest in an affordable home. The fact we could see evidence of Eatonfield's intentions everywhere we looked only made the whole project seem that much more real and exciting.

Back in the UK I was now working on Eatonfield Business Solutions, appointing David Chesters as our Managing Director, an ex-bank manager with more than 35 years experience. My intention was that property developers and business owners could come to us for a tailor-made financial solution to include short and long-term bridging loans, development finance, commercial mortgages, asset finance, cash flow finance, venture capital and funds to enable financial restructuring.

I knew there was a gap in the market for this type of finance, particularly in Wales, so our idea was to become a bridging finance house with Eatonfield providing the opportunity for developers to borrow short-term money. Eatonfield was going to put in between half a million to a £1m to set up the business.

But in 2005 and 2006 I realised I was making more money out of property deals and in the end I decided not to commit to Eatonfield Business Solutions but to stick to the market I knew best. I was also just starting to consider a float on the Alternative Investment Market (AIM) at some time in the future and so I had to be careful where I invested my money; I didn't want to be seen to be diversifying too much. In the end, the timing wasn't right for Eatonfield Business Solutions but I still think it's a good idea and one that I've put on hold rather than abandoned altogether. But if I do return to it, it will be outside the Eatonfield Group. There may, for example, be an opportunity for J's company, The Waterstown Club, to adopt a similar business model and in that respect we may decide to pick up the idea in the not too distant future.

Eatonfield's growth and media coverage resulted in a nomination for the 2005 National Business Awards. We won the Axa Small to Medium Size Business of the Year Award and the Growth Strategy of the Year Award in the prestigious Wales and the West Country regional finals. Gordon Brown, Chancellor of the Exchequer at the time, labelled the awards the 'business Oscars' and Eatonfield was credited as *an outstanding example of a financially and commercially strong business with solid management strategies'*.

That same year, I was a finalist in the Credit Suisse Entrepreneur of the Year which was all very flattering but, controversial as this may sound, I really can't be bothered with award ceremonies. There is a certain amount of publicity and free editorial generated, which is useful of course, but I'd much rather just get on with the next deal than have a panel of 'experts' telling me how well I've done on the last one. As Keith Mather often reminds me I'm forever telling anyone who'll listen that the next deal is important and so, if I can persuade anyone else in the office to attend an award ceremony instead of me then I will, while I get on with the next deal.

Another side effect of our success was that we'd now outgrown our offices at the Old Court House in Holywell, so in November 2005 we sold for £225k - a good rate of return on a building we initially purchased for £40k five years earlier. Eatonfield then bought a £1.25m head office on the Mold business park, moving all 45 members of staff into the office before Christmas. We increased the senior management team appointing Steve Holland as Property Acquisitions Manager and Min Mather, Keith's wife, became our Residential Sales Co-ordinator.

As Min's appointment indicates, Eatonfield had now begun to invest in residential developments as well as commercial but I had no doubt that raising the bar once again wouldn't cause us any problems.

In 2005 and 2006 we exchanged conditional contracts on residential sites and commercial sites including Cwmammon Road Ammanford, a five acre greenfield site suitable for 60 residential units, and the Darren Works factory site at Ystalyfera, earmarked for a further 50 homes.

Commercial developments included the Menzies Distribution Centre at Shepcote Business Park, Sheffield; the former headquarters of Mita Ltd at Bodelwyddan in North Wales; and a 4.5 acre Greenfield site and former caravan park in Carmarthenshire. The contacts we'd built up over the years meant we were now being offered a significant flow of development opportunities in both areas.

Eatonfield Holdings was now more than a successful property company; I considered it to be a successful brand.

We had our own in-house marketing team at Eatonfield's headquarters working closely with Dave Lloyd of Wise Monkey Design.

It was obvious that I was finding time to achieve a lot in business. Sadly, I still hadn't found time to teach H to ride.

CHAPTER ELEVEN

Business solutions; business problems

'Only when the case comes to court will we discover what has happened to the money.'

When it came to our residential developments we made a decision at Eatonfield to concentrate on building fewer, more bespoke properties; we couldn't compete with the big volume builders, so specialisation was key and that's why in 2006 we decided to go 'eco'.

Our affordable house building project in the Bahamas had still not begun, but out of the blue, in January 2006, we were contacted by Jan Ward and informed that 40 plots, or lots as the Bahamians call them, were about to be released to him from the Bahamian Ministry of Housing. At this stage I spoke to Pochin plc, a local Cheshire contractor and informed Anthony Pochin, Construction Director, that if the full contract for the 7,000 properties was won, then Eatonfield would consider a joint venture with his company.

Pochin then paid £350k and Eatonfield £250k into a client

account controlled by Ward and I flew back to Nassau with Anthony and Richard Buck, also of Pochin, and Phil Middlehurst, Eatonfield's Accounts Controller. While we were there, I also took the opportunity to further my own personal plans for a second home when Ward introduced me to Mario Carey. Carey found H and me the perfect lot for our mansion; a spectacular location, right on the beachfront and with beautiful views of the ocean. We were excited at the prospect of our dream holiday home finally taking shape and with that in mind I also transferred £500k personal funds into Ward's client account.

Meanwhile the British government had just announced that all new homes built in the UK would have to be carbon neutral by 2016 which would effectively mean tighter building and planning rules for all residential developments. In December 2006 Communities Secretary, Ruth Kelly, added that by 2050 we should all be aiming for a reduction in carbon emissions by 60%. Given that only a handful of the UK's 160,000 homes built each year is carbon neutral it was an ambitious plan.

Fortunately, Eatonfield was already ahead of the game. We'd already explored a number of ways of building the home of the future, with the intention of introducing a whole range of environmental and energy saving features as standard into our new homes as well as, at a later date, in our commercial developments too. Don't believe any developer who says it's easy to comply with government demands to become carbon neutral; it isn't and I feel perfectly qualified to make that remark because Eatonfield struggled very hard to tick all the boxes, making a few expensive mistakes along the way.

By installing geo-thermal heat pumps, timber windows from sustainable sources, rainwater harvesting and high spec insulation we discovered it was possible to run a four bedroom family home for as little as £150 a year. We believed that we were the first residential developer in Wales to adopt these practices and by stating that we were an eco-friendly house builder it helped smooth the way for our planning applications. Local authorities really wanted to work with us because 'eco' was the buzz word at the time.

In 2006 the residential property market was dominated by major house builders such as Barratts, Taylor Wimpey, Bellway and Redrow. The largest 10 house builders were producing 44% of the output by volume but the tighter planning policy meant that more complex skills were needed to deal with local councils and increasing government legislation. Opportunities for a niche developer such as Eatonfield, who was prepared to develop smaller and more difficult sites for family housing, were there for the taking, all we had to do was apply our expertise.

In 2006 we constructed a small development of seven, four and five bedroom executive-style homes, in four designs at Cwrt Rhyd Galad in Mold which had a total sales value of approximately £3.6m. We were impressed with the construction work of Marrs Davies Ltd, who we'd engaged for the building work, so we bought the company out that year. This meant that Eatonfield was now able to complete the home development circle all in-house, from land purchase through to completion of construction.

But we didn't always get it right. We bought Langley House, again in 2006, an historic mansion near Wilmslow, which had been built as a private home in 1886 but had been used as a corporate headquarters for the last 10 years. We submitted plans to Macclesfield Borough Council outlining our intention to renovate the black and white timbered building to its former glory and convert the outbuildings into a further three properties. We also stated that we wanted to use eco-technology such as ground source heat pumps and rainwater harvesting.

BBC TV's *Working Lunch* heard what we were doing and sent a film crew up to Cheshire to interview Nick Marrs, Eatonfield Homes' Managing Director. The BBC told us we were the first house builder of this type to be featured on the programme and liked the idea of raising the profile of eco-developments. Programme presenter, Simon Gompertz is well known for his enthusiasm for alternative energy and said he would like to re-visit the development to review our progress. Naturally we welcomed the opportunity to showcase what Eatonfield was doing.

In June 2006 we sold the unrenovated main building at Langley House and immediately covered our costs for buying the original seven acre site but what we should have done was sell the whole site.

What I loved about the Langley House project was that it

carried with it a certain amount of kudos and let other niche developers know that Eatonfield was serious – and good at – residential developments. But we lost £1.5m on the development due to overspending on construction costs on the remaining three properties which was completely ridiculous and inexcusable as far as I was concerned.

Other eco-friendly developments included a former dilapidated social club site at Bryn Coed Road in Penmaenmawr where we built six four and five bedroom family homes with a traditional appearance but with very high spec insulation and technology to reduce water usage and energy costs. All the properties were fitted with under floor heating as well as a rainwater harvesting system which recycled filtered rainwater for bathrooms, washing machines and external taps. We submitted similar plans for two further residential plots in Ammanford, south Wales, one for 18 homes and the other for 60.

At the Penmaenmawr development we got even more involved in the eco theme when we donated all the timber from the demolished building to a social enterprise charity for recycling rather than burning it or sending it to a landfill site. I liked the idea that we were helping the environmental lobby. Donating the wood also made commercial sense since the salvage company, 'Against the Grain', sold it on as fencing, garden planters and storage bins.

Eighty tonnes of timber was eventually transported and it made me think what else Eatonfield could donate. I had always been involved in charities to a certain extent, taking part in a number of sponsored events such as fundraising for the Ysbyty Glan Clwyd baby care unit, running for the Dodleston foundation, abseiling for a cancer charity, even donating track suits for the 2007 Rydal rugby tour, but I wanted to get even more involved in charity work in the future, especially if it involved children. It was something I was determined to come back to soon; that and teaching H to ride, of course.

Eatonfield's Development Director, Ian Arnott, got heavily involved in the whole eco-friendly home building policy and became our spokesperson for the media. He explained that there was an option for purchasers to add additional features to an Eatonfield eco-home such as humidity control, solar panels and even mini wind turbines with the result that the heating and cooling system could eventually cost nothing to run.

But the big problem was trying to find the right suppliers for the eco features we wanted to install. Because the technology was new, suppliers weren't all tried and tested and we had our fingers burnt once or twice, especially with the supplier of the ground source heat pumps. As for running costs; yes, £150 per year was very attractive, but at the front end, the extra cost of building these homes had to be added to the selling price with the result that a four bedroom eco home would usually cost an extra £15k to £20k to construct. Not all customers were willing to pay this.

While we were making good progress building houses in

the UK, the Bahamas seemed to have ground to a halt. I knew the idea of building affordable homes in the Bahamas was a good one; in fact it was an excellent idea since in 2005 this was a country with an average family income of $39k yet with a cost of living roughly 50% higher than the US. In the initial stages of discussion I honestly think that Ward had every intention of completing on our deal but he was obviously becoming more and more taken up with the idea of himself as a hot-shot businessman and believed he was a bigger dealmaker than he was; he got carried away and unfortunately, he took Eatonfield and Pochin with him.

Jan Ward was unable to attend our next scheduled meeting so his brother, Monty offered his services instead. Monty was chauffeured all the way from London in a stretch white limo and on arrival we set up the conference call as planned with Pochin's directors, the Ward brothers and Eatonfield all discussing the development opportunity for affordable homes in the Bahamas.

But I was beginning to suspect that all was not well and when I later requested that the systems be put into place for the development to progress there was no response. I became increasingly nervous and when I eventually asked for the return of any monies held in the client account there was no response either. Eventually, all calls I made asking to speak to Jan Ward were ignored. We believed that Ward now had in excess of $2m of client's money in the client account and so I decided I had no other option open to me; I contacted Hammonds, our corporate lawyers in Leeds to instigate proceedings against him.

Three years later the situation is still ongoing with Eatonfield and myself having incurred hundreds of thousands of pounds in legal and professional fees so far.

It appears that the UK principle whereby a client's account is legally established as a safe repository for a client's money simply does not apply in the Bahamas. The local police have since arrested Ward and he's been released on $100k bail with a requirement to report to them once a week making sure he doesn't abscond. Only when the case comes to court will we discover what has happened to the money. I look forward to the outcome because he has caused a lot of anguish for a lot of people.

I'm still awaiting a trial date and looking forward to seeing justice done, not just for my own and Eatonfield's satisfaction, but also for the local Bahamians who trusted him with their money. They believed there was a chance to secure a deposit on their dream home, just as H and I did with our mansion. Jan Ward was very convincing, none of us had any reason to doubt him.

I am disappointed I haven't been able to build my dream home in the Bahamas as the islands are a place of tranquillity with a wonderful quality of life and a resident population that welcomes outsiders. What Eatonfield, Pochin and some of the local Bahamians have been through shows there is another side to paradise.

Following on from our experience, Eatonfield has learnt a tough lesson; we are now even more cautious than before about investing overseas. On a personal level, I am annoyed with myself for letting the whole thing escalate to such a level and I rue the day I ever met Ward. I'd remortgaged our home in the UK to raise the necessary funds for the mansion and now that money is lost to us, pending the results of the trial.

And yet if you were to ask me if I would consider building a home on Paradise Island in the future I would have to say yes. I still think it's one of the most beautiful parts of the world I've ever visited. Unfortunately, H doesn't feel the same way and says she feels physically sick at the thought of going back there. Perhaps when the court case is over and we've put this experience behind us, we can move on. You never know, we may still build the mansion of our dreams in the Bahamas, just not on Paradise Island.

As for Shane Gibson, he was made Immigration Minister in 2005 but resigned in February 2007 when accusations were made regarding his involvement with Anna Nicole Smith. He was photographed, sitting on her bed fully clothed, as he and the model were caught in a close embrace. It was suggested by some that he'd had a personal relationship with her and fast-tracked her application for permanent residency. Whatever the truth of the matter, Shane Gibson stepped down from his position as a result of the scandal.

The latest news is that he's been re-elected, this time as an opposition member as his party, the Free National Movement, recently lost the election.

In the middle of all this I was about to raise the bar even higher; I wanted to float Eatonfield on the Alternative Investment Market, commonly known as AIM. This was the one project that was to test me to my limits but I had no doubt in my mind that it was the right thing to do for the company.

CHAPTER TWELVE

'Aim-ing' high

'I was now the chief executive of a publicly listed company.'

While our legal firm, Hammonds, continued with our case against Ward I turned my attention to floating the company. I had a good land bank, profitable developments and an excellent team of people around me; not only were my managers good at their jobs they were all highly qualified members of their respective professions, in fact I was the only senior member of staff with no letters after my name. What I needed now was an injection of cash. On a personal level I also needed a return on the investment I'd made in Eatonfield over the years, but more importantly I needed money to grow the business. I also continued to hold on to my dream of one day owning my own stables. As anyone in the racing world will tell you, you need an awful lot of cash to do that and I wanted to compete with the best in the business; I wanted to own the biggest and best yard outside Newmarket. That sort of ambition doesn't come cheap, but what I didn't know at this stage was just how expensive it was going to be.

My intention was to raise £5m for my personal ambitions and £10m for growing the business. Jill Jones, Senior Partner at the Chester office of Baker Tilly, Eatonfield's accountants and auditors for the build up to the float, got to know me very well in the period leading up to the big day and probably summed me up after just one meeting.

"You're not a details man, are you Rob?" she said.

I've always been better at looking at the bigger picture and I've always been ambitious. I think big, but I also work hard and it didn't take Jill long to understand that my ambition was firmly grounded in reality. Soon she was putting Eatonfield's accounts and administration through its paces, commenting that *'my optimism was contagious'*. Fortunately, we had a lot more going for us than optimism.

In the six months to November 2006 I was working 14 to 16 hour days; I rarely saw H or the children and was spending most of my time at corporate meetings, yet I still had to run Eatonfield at the same time. We made one or two changes to Eatonfield's personnel along the way, with the appointment of Terry Carroll as Group Finance Director probably the most important. Carroll joined us in August 2006 bringing with him more than 36 years of financial and management experience. His previous roles included treasurer of the Halifax and financial director and CEO of N&P. He had the added advantage of having led flotation projects in the past. Phil Middlehurst remained as Accounts

Controller but didn't have the necessary professional qualifications to take us through the float and unfortunately it became clear pretty quickly that Carroll and Phil didn't always see eye-to-eye.

We appointed Evolution as our corporate advisers and broker, with David Armitage, Head of Corporate Law at Hammonds, as our legal adviser. David's technical fluency and commercial approach was second to none and he put together a team to go through every page of our flotation document, checking every statement, verifying every word and making sure that the qualifications of our senior management team were of the necessary standard for a limited company.

We then appointed Savills to provide up-to-date valuations of all the properties we held in our portfolio at the time.

The preparation for the float took nine months in total and almost £1m in fees.

The admission document was finally approved once Evolution and I had decided just how much I wanted to dilute the company. We agreed on an issue of 23 million shares with the value based on a multiplier of earnings rather than a net asset value. We decided to go out at a slight discount; and set the price at 125p a share. Eatonfield's market capitalisation was just under £30m and I wanted to retain 48% of the business.

The next stage of the flotation process was the road show where we presented to more than 30 institutions in two weeks, visiting London, Glasgow, Edinburgh, Geneva, Birmingham and Leeds; in each case we had a 20 minute window of opportunity to present to the fund managers who all took reams of notes and bombarded us with questions. It was clear straight away that what these fund managers didn't like was the founder of the business taking cash out, under the assumption that he or she was then going to take the money and spend the next 20 years sitting on a beach. They wanted a commitment from the founder, so I gave an assurance that I would not sell any of my shares in Eatonfield for at least two years.

The share price of 125p was an attractive one and we knew we would get the issue away at that price, but it just needed one big name to come forward. At the end of the first week you get a pretty clear idea of who's interested and who isn't but everyone still sits on the fence. What Evolution tried to do was to get someone on board as a corner stone investor but it's the hardest job; every investor wants to know who else is interested before they commit.

Then after one particular meeting with GAM investment managers it all started to fall into place. GAM turned to Evolution and said they were interested in investing in the company. We could now say to other fund managers; "The order book's filling up, here's your chance to buy into a strong company, don't leave it too long before committing."

UBS then said that they were also interested. Fund managers started talking to one another and word spread, building up the order book.

Next thing we knew; following our presentation in Geneva, SAAD Investment Company announced it wanted it wanted to take the maximum shares allowed: 29.9%, which was a coup to say the least. The Geneva-based operation is part of the bigger SAAD Group, based in Bahrain, which has interests in a diverse range of companies from engineering to health, from education to real estate and has approx €10.4bn total funds under management. As a result, every fund manager suddenly sat up and took notice which was fantastic news for us - until Pochin plc made an announcement.

Pochin had no intention of waiting any longer for their money, which was supposedly lying in the client's account in the Bahamas and stated they were about to instruct their solicitors. Carroll panicked and instead of being supportive he almost blamed me for the situation. As if things weren't stressful enough, I now had to start defending myself in front of my FD which, I have to say, was one of the worst experiences of my professional career. Carroll knew Eatonfield had to be seen to be whiter than white for the float to succeed, but so did I. He was extremely worried about the stigma attached to any possible repercussions. and said we may have to pull the float if matters weren't resolved in the Bahamas. I was not about to throw away everything I'd worked so hard for during the last eight years for some Bahamian businessman - and I made that very clear to Carroll. He countered with the argument that the publicity generated by Pochin's possible court case could damage us. I knew that Carroll was not the sort of man who took risks; in fact I admired him for his methodical and steady approach but, at the same time, I wasn't about to give up. There had to be a way round the problem.

And there was. I was eventually able to come to an agreement with Pochin, effectively paying them one third of the £350k they had lodged with Ward and the float was able to proceed. We'd come through the panic – just - but I knew that my relationship with my Financial Director was irreparably damaged in the process.

We decided to stick with our original intention to split the shares, with a single investor limited to a maximum of 29.9% with SAAD announcing it would take as much as possible. We knew then we were on to a winner.

With most company flotations, a broker will use a fund manager's interest as a lever to encourage commitment and to place a deadline on closing the order book. Evolution kept the book running and we were eventually oversubscribed.

Shares started trading on 18th November at 125p and rose throughout the day to close at 134.5p. I watched the process with the rest of Eatonfield's staff on screen at our head office in Mold, some colleagues having taken up the offer of buying share options themselves and I couldn't help reflecting for a moment on my life and how far I'd come since living in the caravan in North Wales.

Eight years ago I had absolutely nothing to my name; no assets, no home and no money. Today I had just floated a company I'd started in 1998 which was valued at £28.75m. I was about to realise £5m in cash and invest £10m of our new shareholders money back into the company. I was proud of what we'd all achieved at Eatonfield and so was Sam.

In 2007 Sam wasn't in good health; he was suffering from emphysema following years of heavy smoking and the hard physical work he'd had to do on the farm hadn't done him any favours either. He now lived with us at Fron Farm where H and I could keep an eye on him but he didn't get out much, other than to a couple of pubs not too far from Halkyn.

Nan and Teddy West had died more than ten years ago but I could still see Nan slipping me the occasional fiver or £10 for a bet on a horse; it was a pity I couldn't slip her a few back, and as for my grandmother, Margaret, she was still living with her daughter, Gill, in Widnes where I'm pretty sure she was able to understand the significance of the float, even at the age of 97. I thought back to the name of the original family business; M A Lloyd & Son, when Margaret Alice Lloyd would take charge of all the accounts and admin at Flash Farm and I didn't doubt for one minute that running a business must run in the blood.

Frank was watching it all from his office in London. "Your turn for lunch, then," he said, when he 'phoned later that day, which was rich since I was pretty sure I'd bought lunch the last three times we'd met.

All of my family had helped me in their own way and

they'd all been an inspiration to me. I hoped I could now be an inspiration for them. But first I took a moment to let the full realisation at what I'd just achieved sink in: I was now the chief executive of a publicly listed company.

That night H and I went out for a quiet meal and I could tell she had something on her mind. "I hope this doesn't mean you'll have to carry on working 16 hour days, Rob," she said, looking at me with a mixture of pride and concern.

"I don't think so, nothing could be as tough as the last six months," I said, naively.

In fact 16 hour days soon became the norm.

I didn't have time to dwell on my achievement for long as it became obvious just how different my role in Eatonfield was about to become and, if I'm completely honest, I didn't enjoy it for the first 12 months. I still had to put together the deals but now I had the added responsibility of dealing with the shareholders as well. I was the chief point of contact and this was all new ground for me. I got used to it eventually, but there was no getting away from the fact that my hands were tied. In the past if I wanted to do a deal I could do it with minimal consent, but now I had to have a board meeting. A good example of the increased accountability was cheque runs; two signatories were now required, whereas in the past it was only my signature that mattered. And of course Eatonfield would not automatically go for a development just because I thought it was a good one; it had to have the full agreement of the board.

Eatonfield Group plc became the holding company; Eatonfield Developments owned all of the assets. In accordance with the rules we appointed two non-executive directors. Sir Leslie Young, ex-Chairman and Managing Director of J. Bibby and Sons plc from 1968 to 1985, was appointed Eatonfield's non-executive Chairman. Sir Leslie was also a main board director with Nat West Bank from 1979 to 1989 and Director of the Bank of England from 1984 to 1988 as well as a non-executive Director of Granada Television. He had further contacts with the Northwest having been appointed as the inaugural Chairman of the Merseyside Development Corporation from 1980 to 1984 and Chairman of National Museums and Galleries on Merseyside from 1986 to 1995.

Suki Kalirai was also appointed non-executive Director. Suki graduated from Imperial College in 1980 with a degree in Chemistry and held senior positions with Coca-Cola and Forte Hotels, later becoming Chairman of Serve Health and Beauty Ltd, the largest independent operator of day spa and beauty salons in the UK. He was also Chairman and a director of the Spa Business Association and a non-executive Director of the Hair and Beauty Industry Authority.

I was Group Chief Executive and Terry Carroll was Group Finance Director. Eatonfield's senior management team consisted of Ian Arnott, Development Director; Mike Baker, Banking Co-ordinator and Group Treasurer; Steve

Holland, Acquisitions Manager; Steve Jones, Design Manager; Nick Marrs, Contracts Director; Keith Mather, Legal Director; Phil Middlehurst, Accounts Director; and Jonathan Richards, Land Director. Most of the senior management team had been with Eatonfield for a long time; Keith Mather from the very beginning. Board meetings were scheduled for once a quarter, or once a month, to make sure we were on top of the corporate governance.

In 2007 our share price reached a high of 190p. With the £10m investment we expanded at a rapid rate, opening offices in Bristol, Cardiff and Newcastle. We appointed Simon de Vere as land and regeneration Director in Newcastle with specific responsibility for development opportunities on both greenfield and brownfield sites and in both commercial and residential sectors. In Bristol, Neil Turley was appointed Director of Commercial Developments.

My ambition for Eatonfield Group plc focused on securing significant land holdings to grow the business in all these areas and, more importantly perhaps, the board agreed with me.

CHAPTER THIRTEEN

Buying the Bentley

'Part of our expertise lay in working out the masterplan, acquiring suitable planning permission and then selling on to the bigger housebuilders.'

We floated in November 2006 and in December 2006 H and I visited the Bentley factory in Crewe to choose my long awaited and long desired luxury car.

We were driven to the factory from the showroom in Manchester where a member of staff led us through the on-site museum, past the display of early Bentley cars and then into the workshop. I remember feeling incredibly excited but I also felt an overwhelming sense of achievement. This was it; I could actually afford to buy a Bentley of my own, the car I had imagined driving for so long. I thought back to the days when Sam would drive me up and down the country in Tony Carter's Mondeo and then back a bit further to when I had no car at all. And then I shuddered at the memory of sitting in the shed in the car park at Albion Street. The muddy patch of land was still there, tucked in behind Habitat and still crowded with cars paying by the day or by the hour but, thank God, someone else was sitting in the wooden hut now, taking the money.

I took H's hand as we watched the engineers sanding down the metalwork, peering at the finish for the slightest imperfection before they started on the first layer of paint. These luxury cars are still produced in the same factory that has been synonymous with the Bentley brand for nearly 70 years. In terms of production a Bentley is produced in six months unlike the usual assembly line vehicles which take just two days on average and every single one is built to order. For £200k you can choose the car of your dreams and as part of that dream H and I chose the dashboard, the wheels, the colour of the leather on the seats, the steering wheel and the colour of the paint. Most procedures are performed by hand and it takes a full three weeks to assemble the body; eight days to apply the paint.

"What colour would you like?" asked H.

"That depends on which colour is most popular," I replied and H looked at me with raised eyebrows.

"Don't you want to choose something different?" she asked. "This is the car of your dreams after all; you could make it distinctive."

But I was too busy thinking of the resale value. In my opinion it was better to have the subtle two-tone silver grey than anything that would frighten the horses.

The Bentley was ready just before Christmas and I duly arrived at the factory in Crewe to pick it up and bring it home. It was a miserable wet day and I was just coming off the A55, preparing to drive the last few miles to Fron Farm, when a stone hit the windscreen. I sat there at the junction, completely deflated, looking at the small but distinctive chip in the top right hand corner, then I called the factory, took it back and paid £1,500 to have it replaced.

Finally, finally, I had the car; all I needed now was the chauffeur so I asked Jan Bailey, my PA, to put an advert in the local paper and watched the applications roll in; more than 100 in total.

I knew I could trust Jan to choose the most suitable candidate so I left that task to her; not only was she extremely good at her job, she could practically read my mind. Years spent working together meant she knew what I needed before I did and in the darker days, when the property market took a downturn and we had to make redundancies, she was probably the member of staff I missed the most.

Paul Ditchfield was 39 years old and had been a chauffeur at United Utilities for 20 years until he'd been made redundant a couple of months earlier. He'd prepared his CV and instead of posting it had driven to Eatonfield's offices in Mold, a round trip of 60 miles from his home near Warrington, to hand it over in person. Jan told me that Paul arrived, dressed in a suit and tie as if he was already anticipating an interview. "I was just passing," he said, not too convincingly. "And I thought I'd drop this off rather than trust the post." Paul stayed for a chat and obviously made an impression because before you could say, 'Turn left at the next junction' he was on Jan's short list.

The following week I called Paul in and settled down for the interview with Terry Carroll.

"I see you've passed the advanced driving course," I said by way of introduction and Paul said that yes, he had, and then went on to give me details of the anti-terrorist driving course that had also been part of his training, the number of times he'd taken the chairman of United Utilities to London, and how well he knew the road system in most of the cities in the UK. Paul Ditchfield sounded to me like the ideal chauffeur for Eatonfield.

Our FD took a slightly different approach. "Tell me about yourself, Paul, I want to know all about you."

"What do you want to know about me for?" asked Paul. "I've told you all about my driving qualifications. I can tell you all about Eatonfield if you want." He'd obviously done a bit of research on us and wanted to show off his knowledge, but Carroll wasn't interested.

"No Paul; I want to hear all about you, The Man. I want to know what makes you tick; go on Paul; tell me." Paul didn't look away, although to be fair, he did look a bit puzzled, especially when Carroll continued with the combative approach. "All I've got to do is ask you five questions, Paul, as a result of which you'll be in tears. What do you make of that?"

Paul looked at Eatonfield's Financial Director long and hard. "I can make you cry too," he replied. "All I've got to do is knee you in the ..."

"Right," I said firmly, putting a stop to their exchange.

I'd heard enough. Carroll's strange interviewing technique aside, I knew that Paul was the man for the job.

Paul Ditchfield and I make a good team; we both love the Bentley; it's comfortable, luxurious and has everything I've ever dreamed of in a car but even with the added benefit of Paul – or Ditch as I call him - at the wheel, the car has done just 15,000 miles in two years. I won't deny that it's wonderful to drive to the races in style and cruise luxuriously to a parking spot next to the owner's enclosure, or be transported in comfort to London for a meeting, but I think it's a bit over the top to bring to work every day.

It also has a curious habit of whistling when you drive faster than 70mph. Ditch tells me it's a design quirk of the car – I hesitate to call it a fault.

There are two knobs on the traditionally designed dashboard that when pulled towards you allow air to circulate. As soon as the Bentley picks up speed you can hear the air whistling through the vents so I sent the car back to Crewe and while the engineers looked at it I was given a Rolls Royce Silver Spur which is also a lovely car, but in my view doesn't have quite the same status as the Bentley. Unfortunately, the whistling persists, so all I can do is make sure that Ditch sticks to the speed limit at all times.

People have asked me: 'Why a Bentley?' and I have to say that it's an experience I wouldn't have missed for anything. The car has an enormous 'feel-good' factor. If I've had a difficult week, I can sit at the wheel, take the family out for Sunday lunch and feel that all's right with the world. It lifts you. But for day-to-day driving I stick with the Range Rover; it's more practical.

So, in order to justify the expense of the car and just to prove that owning a Bentley really did help me 'do the bigger deal' I wasted no time in raising the bar again. We were now a public company and as we were perceived to be bigger, we were offered bigger deals; deals that we hadn't come across before. The publicity generated from the float meant our name travelled further afield: Prior to 2006 many people hadn't heard of Eatonfield outside Wales but we were now appearing more and more frequently in the national press. City institutions would contact us as a regional player and instead of being offered deals of half a million pounds it was now £10m or £20m.

One of the fastest, most satisfying deals of my whole career was the 24 acre Bookham Technology site in Paignton which Eatonfield bought just after the float for £5m. In June 2007 we sold the site for £10.075m to Modus, with the sale structured so that Eatonfield were in a 50% profit share agreement with the Manchester-based developer to take the project forward and benefit from any future development gains or any profit arising from an earlier sale.

Naturally, I was delighted; it was well above our projected targeted price and the fact we had an interest in any future development only made it more successful. Today, in 2009, Modus and Eatonfield are still talking to other interested parties, one of them being the supermarket giant, Asda.

That same year we agreed an option on the 47 acre Carless oil refinery site, part of the Clydebank Urban Regeneration Masterplan; a multi-million pound mixed use development with residential making up the bulk of the development and offices and retail the remaining 20%. The site is in an attractive natural setting, with panoramic views over the river, west towards the Erskine Bridge and north to the hills above Old Kirkpatrick. The western part was previously a shipbuilding yard, active during both world wars and produced many naval and merchant vessels. The eastern side was an oil storage facility and a depot remained on site until at least 1989.

The Carless development is still ongoing; there is a huge decontamination cost attached to the land and we still have the option to buy. Even in today's market we have every intention of forging ahead with the development and we expect a response regarding Eatonfield's plans sometime in the first half of 2009.

The whole Carless site is currently vacant and the masterplan is at a preliminary stage but once development gets under way it will be a particularly significant investment for us.

It is also one of two important brownfield sites that Eatonfield is involved with at the moment, the other being one of Eatonfield's biggest developments to date; the Corus Steel Works site in Workington. This is a £180m mixed development for which we've submitted plans to include a day care nursery, an hotel, leisure facilities, a care village for the elderly, conference centre, pub, promenade and 600 residential units. Eatonfield is using its expertise to the full and in the process hoping to breathe new life into this dilapidated, run-down former steelworks site.

As you can imagine, I expected a lot of interest in Eatonfield's plans for the Corus site but I didn't realise how keen that interest would be.

I walked into the first planning meeting in mid 2007 expecting to be greeted by just one or two members from Allerdale Borough Council, only to be met by a total of 28 interested parties from economic development, to highways engineers, to the police, all keen to hear Eatonfield's plans for the 87 acres. We'd labelled this particular development 'a community within a community' with affordable homes included in the plans and, at the time we exchanged on the site, we had at least a dozen national house builders interested in getting involved: Persimmon, Barratt and Taylor Wimpey were all waiting in the wings just waiting for the plans to be approved.

We appointed Knight Frank to lead the planning application, supported by McCormick Architecture, Enviros Consulting, Joynes Pike & Associates Ltd, Gleeds and David Daniell Associates. Everything was in place to take the project forward.

The Corus site has a history stretching back 120 years and is obviously very important to the people of west Cumbria.

The site was home to the Moss Bay steelworks which at its peak employed 5,000 people. By 2006 only 38 workers remained on site; a vivid illustration of the changing fortunes of west Cumbria if ever there was one. We expect the mixed use development to be a great boost to the area providing jobs, housing and recreation facilities and we weren't the only ones who believed that. Workington MP Tony Cunningham said: "The development of the Corus site is a huge opportunity for both Eatonfield and for the community of West Cumbria. The potential for job creation and economic growth is tremendous. I am delighted that Eatonfield want to work with the people of West Cumbria to bring long term success in the area."

And I couldn't agree more, except perhaps to say that I believe the development of the Corus site could literally be a once in a lifetime opportunity to transform Workington.

But make no mistake; it's also a big opportunity for Eatonfield. A brownfield site of this importance can generate a return of up to 200%. On residential sites Eatonfield looks for a return of 20%, with commercial, 25% but with brownfield sites, the usual rules of developing don't apply. The big problem for the developer is the work you've got to do before building can start on the site since decontamination is often an issue and not all developers are skilled in this area.

In 2009 the value of land per acre varied widely; agricultural land was approximately £3k an acre, industrial £100k and residential up to £400k. If plans are approved for a supermarket on a development site, the cost per acre jumps to £1.5m. But today's developer needs to factor in the turnover period from acquiring brownfield land to selling it. This period has increased, on average, from six months to two years, due mainly to the more detailed reports that all developers now have to submit.

So, in 2007, bearing in mind the effect that developing brownfield sites was having on our cashflow, we made a decision to expand the residential side of our business. We wanted to move away from what I would call 'bulky deals'; by which I mean the big commercial developments, as the money often took a long time to come in, resulting in inconsistent cash flow. The idea was to stop the lumpiness over a 12 month period since with house building the cash flow is much more fluid.

When it came to residential developments we had our own distinctive set of criteria that we followed to maximise profit and ensure a high standard of build. We always took a flexible approach with each residential development we got involved in; if we wanted a quick profit, we'd sell, but, by the same token, we knew we could also develop the site out if we chose to since we had our own in-house construction team, Marrs Davies.

However, by the end of 2007/early 2008 the market was starting to dip and Eatonfield decided to take a strategic view and slow the residential developments down. At this stage in the game we had become well known as a trader of sites, skilled in working through planning applications.

Part of our expertise lay in working out the master plan for the site, obtaining suitable planning permission and then selling on to the big house builders. Residential developers such as Taylor Wimpey or Barratts want what is known in the trade as 'oven-ready sites'. For them, getting planning consents is nothing more than a financial problem. They want delivered sites and that's exactly what Eatonfield had become expert at; the planning aspect of developing. We're also very good at buying at the right price and as the market became tougher and tougher, we had to concentrate at what we were best at in order to survive.

Interestingly, the growth period for Eatonfield, immediately after the float, made me think long and hard about those who were less fortunate than me. I was very grateful for my success and I certainly didn't take it for granted. I knew I'd worked hard to get where I was today but my success was also partly due to the fact that I'd been given opportunities and grasped them with both hands. I knew full well that there were some people out there who never had those opportunities so, when the chance came for me to set aside time to help others, I jumped at it.

CHAPTER FOURTEEN

Charity begins at a Romanian home

'I thought of the homeless teenagers in Chester sinking or swimming in the same situation.'

It was early one morning at the beginning of 2007 and I was standing at our bedroom window at home, looking out at the Dee Estuary as it glistened under a silvery-grey, winter's sun and I remember thinking how lucky I was to have all of this; H, three healthy children, my home and my business. Life couldn't get much better. But it also made me think about others who weren't so fortunate. What about those who didn't have a loving family and what about everyone out there who didn't have a warm and welcoming home to go to? I thought about the time I'd been walking the streets of Chester when I had no job myself and the homeless youngsters I saw doing their best to survive. Over the years I've lost weight and a full head of hair for good causes. Helen had persuaded me to shave my head for the Glan Clwyd Hospital's baby care unit not long after we met and I lost two stone and gained £2,000 for a sponsored slim as a fund raiser for a children's hospital. I also helped raise funds for the four-man Welsh darts team in 2003 when they needed money for their trip to France for the World Championships. I felt it was time now to make more of a commitment to a good cause and in February 2007 the opportunity presented itself.

Horizon Children's Charity was based in Connah's Quay and was set up by George Woodworth and Harry Eakins to help disabled children and young adults in Romania. These children had no families and had spent most of their lives in state-run orphanages, soulless institutions that had sprung up around Romania as a result of President Ceausescu's disastrous policies in the late 1980s. Disabilities ranged from deafness to learning difficulties, from missing limbs to mental health problems, all conditions which meant that when it came to adoption, these children were usually last on the list.

The situation in Romania hit the headlines in the UK for the first time in 1990. The whole world was stunned by images of malnourished and unloved children and babies, confined to these 'orphanages' where staff were simply too overworked and underfunded to respond to their needs. The children were starving, freezing and in some cases chained to their beds. The unnatural sound of silence that permeated the buildings was simply because the children had learnt that no-one came to their aid if they cried; so they would lie there without a sound all day, every day.

In fact, the children often weren't orphans at all but the

product of unwanted pregnancies. Ceausescu had banned contraception for all women in Romania until they'd produced at least five children but his policies meant that they were too poor to feed or clothe these extra babies so they would take them to these prison-like institutions and leave them there. There was no shame attached to their actions because so many people were doing it; it became almost normal.

When the world's media discovered this lost generation of children there was a scramble from all four corners of the globe to offer homes for the abandoned orphans. Only the disabled children were ignored and that's where the Horizon Children's Charity came in. George told us that once these youngsters reached the age of 18 or 19 they were kicked out of the institutions in which they'd been raised. Many end up as 'street children', stealing to survive or getting involved in drugs and prostitution. It was a grim existence and one that was impossible to get out of until 1993 when Henrik Haubro and Sebastian Ghita provided a glimmer of hope when they established the Helios Foundation. Their vision of a better life for these young people resulted in the setting up of European House, a collection of buildings that provides living accommodation for up to 60 residents who are either severely disabled or who have HIV.

European House, situated in Romania's second city, Craiova, has been built with donations and with help from the Romanian authorities. It consists of flats, apartments and two farms where the residents are taught how to lead self sufficient lives. Horizon Children's Charity supported the institution for many years before H and I got involved and in the early days it was one of the poorest institutions of its kind in Romania but with the charity's support it gradually became one of the best in the country. I was interested and wanted to know more.

I spoke to George Woodworth and asked him how much money the charity needed for European House and I believe the answer was 'bottomless.' I explained the situation to H and she immediately decided she would organise a series of fund raising events with a black tie charity dinner at the Chester Grosvenor planned for 30th March 2007. We aimed to raise £10k via ticket sales, a charity auction, sponsorship and a grand raffle and after discussing it with George decided that the money would be best used to support and renovate the placement centres at European House, help with the centre for the deaf, clean and maintain the water wells and sponsor experienced carers to look after the disabled.

In February Helen and I packed our bags for Romania to see the situation for ourselves. We were going to be offered a tour of European House in Craiova to see where any money we pledged would be used, in the meantime we'd already suggested that everyone at our head office in Mold should get involved too and a month earlier the Horizon Children's Charity had been nominated as Eatonfield's charity of the year.

On Thursday 8th February H and I flew to Bucharest where we were met by Sebastian Ghita and his assistant Simona.

"We are so happy to see you," said Sebastian, shaking our hands warmly. Sebastian was well set, balding and had a smooth, round face; he looked the sort who'd be happier giving you a bear hug than a handshake. He also struck me as reliable. In fact, everything I've learnt about him since the day we met only confirms that initial impression.

His assistant Simona spoke good English and greeted us confidently. "We are happy to find you here," she said, "We hope your visit will determine that you continue to help these young people in the future."

H and I said we would do everything we could to help and followed them both to the car.

Four hours later we arrived in the city of Craiova. "It's so...grey," whispered Helen.

"Grey and depressing," I said, looking at the buildings, which all looked industrial and utilitarian. Electricity cables hung overhead like empty washing lines. It wasn't a glamorous city that's for sure, but then it wasn't a glamorous trip.

After supper in our hotel, Sebastian and Simona left us alone to absorb everything we'd experienced so far. We were scheduled to meet Gheorghe Barbarasa, the Secretary of the county council, the next morning at 10am, after which Sebastian and Simona would take us to visit the places and people who would be benefiting from our money. H and I were looking forward to it, but we were also slightly apprehensive.

"What if it's so upsetting we don't want to come again?" said H.

"I'm sure it won't be that bad," I said. "Don't forget; we're here to help and that's the most important thing."

I might have sounded confident but I didn't feel it. H could be right; what if we were overwhelmed by the scale of the problem in Romania when we saw it up close? Communicating via email was one thing, but actually meeting the disabled residents of European House was another matter altogether.

After our brief meeting with Gheorghe the next morning, Sebastian and Simona filled our two days from early in the morning to seven in the evening with visits to the centre for the deaf, the farm, European House, the art museum and a city tour.

One resident we met made a particular impression; 32-year-old Aurel Filip, sole carer for Alexandru and Nicolae Tudor, two severely disabled brothers. The brothers, who were both in wheelchairs, couldn't walk, eat or do the simplest tasks without Aurel's help. Before they came to European House the boys had had a grim existence with little or no stimulation. Then in 2005 the charity had paid for them to spend six months in Denmark where they'd attended a specialist school that had helped them to improve their communication skills. Back in Romania Aurel had continued with the good work.

"Aurel says they are happy to live together," said Simona translating for us as Aurel described his day. "They all are living here in one of the apartment with four other boys," she added.

H and I looked at the immaculate lounge and kitchen. The rooms were basic but they were spotless.

"And how can we help?" I asked looking from Simona and Aurel to Alexandru and Nicolae.

"We would like to pay Aurel a wage since he is officially a carer for the boys," explained Sebastian. "But we do not have the funds."

"How much would a monthly wage be for someone like Aurel?" I asked.

"£110," said Sebastian.

It seemed a small amount for such an important job and H and I wordlessly nodded our agreement.

We then moved on to visit the school for the deaf where once again we were greeted warmly. The teachers were keen to show us the work displayed on the walls, particularly the embroideries and engravings which were used as a tool for the pupils to improve their hand co-ordination.

Our overriding impression was a lack of resources but that didn't seem to bother the children; on the whole they were smiling and happy. We looked at the cracked windows, the bare concrete floors and the ramshackle desks and chairs in every room and our hearts sank.

"Is the problem too big for us to tackle?" whispered Helen as we followed Simona and Sebastian from room to room. "We'd need to invest millions to bring this place up to the standard of a British school."

I nodded; totally dismayed at the lack of any home comforts everywhere we looked. Only the staff raised our spirits; they were totally dedicated and selfless, full of patience and with a kindness that you just don't see in everyday life. I think it was the commitment of the staff that convinced me to stay and hear more.

Some of the rooms in this building appeared to be out of bounds and Sebastian explained that we were not allowed access. H and I wondered if the more troubled residents were housed in these areas; disabled individuals considered too distressing for us to see. Our scheduled visit to the Saint Andrei placement centre was also cancelled and we wondered if it was for the same reason. Perhaps it was for the best, who knows? On one level we could understand why we were protected from the truth; on the other, we would have liked the full picture. Nevertheless, this tour made clear that our money was necessary, especially when we saw the state of the living accommodation.

The next day, Sebastian and Simona showed us Tatomiresti Farm, which was more of a smallholding than an actual farm. The residents here had livestock and grew their own vegetables and fruit and it all looked very encouraging until we saw the run down block of apartments standing forlornly in the centre.

"These flats don't look habitable," said H as she glanced at the decaying plaster on the walls and witnessed the

David Hanson MP at the official opening of our new head office in Mold

Eatonfield's new website with left-right, Steve Jones, Steve Holland, Mike Baker, Paul Noal and Min Mather

The best day ever!, J, me, H, Jo and Dan, just perfect

Jo, the apple of my eye

An action packed day out with Jo, H Dan & J

Terry and Eileen Washer have been firm friends of ours for many years. Their racehorse, American Champ, is stabled at Rob Lloyd Racing

Mac and Jan Mcleod, two of my closest friends who stable both their racehorses, More Tea Vicar and Moneysupermarket with Rob Lloyd Racing

Here with Mandy and Nicola Smith of Kiss PR

The 'Haycroft Team' at Rob Lloyd Racing

With Bloodstock agent, Bobby O'Ryan who has a keen eye for a winner

Channel 4's Mike Cattermole at the official opening of Rob Lloyd Racing

April 2008, Haycroft Farm starts to take shape

With Mac and Simon Nixon CEO of moneysupermarket.com with horse named Moneysupermarket

With Dan, Ricky Hatton, Nathan and his dad Tom

In Belfast with Andrew Mulvenna and Lucy from The Secret Millionaire

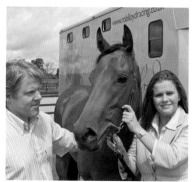

With Oceanic Dancer and Kerry Katona

Big Brother's Lisa Appleton and Mario Marconi with their horse Bebenine

*Suzanne Collins and me with
Anacot Steel*

Nick Hancock and H with Honey Berry

*With Phil Bennett and Sir Henry Cooper at J's charity fund raising event
for his trip to the Sinai Desert*

H, my beautiful soul mate

barely functioning plumbing.

"But they could easily be made habitable," I said. I was already making a mental inventory of the work required to bring the property up to scratch. This was something I understood; this was where I would feel happy putting our money, in fact I was looking forward to offering advice on the whole renovation project from start to finish. At last, I felt H and I could make a difference. I'd done this sort of thing countless times before and I wanted to do it again now.

"This is a chance for people to become self sufficient after a lifetime in an institution," explained Sebastian as he introduced us to Luminata Ene who had been in an orphanage all of his life and had severe learning difficulties. Barely six months ago, this thirty-three year old didn't even know how to make a cup of tea, but the staff at European House had patiently taught him how to plant vegetables, cook a meal, even how to milk a cow.

"This is great; this is definitely a worthwhile project," I said to H with conviction. It made perfect sense to me to fund a development project on this smallholding in Craiova because this was a place where a lost generation of Romanians were being given all the tools to help themselves.

After what H and I had seen we were under no illusions; we knew the problem in Craiova was a big one but we didn't think it was insurmountable. We went back to Romania twice in total, each time seeing evidence of where our money was being spent and noting small improvements along the way. We saw Aurel, Alexandru, Nicolae and Luminata and others like them making steady improvement and we took photographs and stories back with us to Eatonfield as we planned a full programme of fund raising.

In March we went ahead with our planned charitable dinner at the Chester Grosvenor Hotel. Retired premier league referee, Jeff Winter, gave a great after dinner speech and colleague, Peter Stevenson entertained us with his jazz band. Everyone agreed that it was a fabulous night. The money raised was used to support and renovate the apartment block where the young adults were being rehoused and at the same time I tried to offer as much advice as I could with the practicalities of renovating the run-down buildings. A sum was also set aside for cleaning and maintenance of the water wells. Horizon Children's Charity in Connah's Quay was very grateful as were Simona and Sebastian. We sent money for bathrooms, furniture, wages, general renovations, even food.

Our daughter Jo also got involved. She helped H organise the ball at The Grosvenor and then visited Romania herself as part of Gordonstoun's nominated charity. We all wanted nothing more than to make a difference but H and I were under no illusions, we knew we were only scratching the surface and after a while a nagging thought began to take hold.

"You might have been right," I said one evening back at Fron Farm. "I think the situation in Romania might be too big for us." I'd also recently decided that I wanted more control over where the money was being spent as I was worried that the renovation project was not being run as tightly as I would have liked. I knew I was good at adding value to any development I worked on and I couldn't help wanting to do the same in Romania.

Twelve months later H and I eventually made the decision that we had done as much as we could for European House. I'd offered money and expertise and I hoped it had been useful in helping to build a life for these disabled young people but I made a decision that any future charity I was going to get involved in would have to be closer to home. I wanted more input and I wanted to feel part of the day-to-day operation.

Not long after we'd forwarded our last donation to European House, Channel 4 contacted me and asked if I would like to appear on the programme, *Secret Millionaire*. Given what I'd experienced so far with charity work, I was keen to do more. Unfortunately, it was clear to me that H didn't feel the same way.

CHAPTER FIFTEEN

Horses and Haycroft

'I made the mistake of trying to gallop before I could walk.'

As Jason had so aptly put it: "Property and horses are in Dad's blood" - and I couldn't agree more. There's nothing to compare with the feeling of doing a deal like the Bookham deal or winning with a horse that you've bought, trained and coaxed until its race fit. It's a mixture of happiness and sheer excitement that lifts you to another level. Once you've had that feeling you can't wait for it to happen again; it's addictive, just like a drug.

Even before I floated Eatonfield I'd owned racehorses and on 6th August 2006 I achieved what many horse lovers and owners in Cheshire can only dream about; I had a winner at Chester racecourse.

Known as the Roodee, Chester racecourse is situated on what used to be the Roman settlement of the city and is the oldest course in the country. Every meeting draws huge crowds with visitors streaming in from all parts of the UK, converging on the city's narrow cobbled streets and walking along the famous Roman rows. I love the buzz of a day at the races, with hats and high heels everywhere you look. H likes me to join in the fashion parade with a tailored suit, striped shirt and a silk tie and I don't mind making an effort; it makes a change from the ancient pair of jeans and orange string belt that I pull on at weekends.

The Roodee is one of only two racecourses in the UK in the centre of a city, the other is York, and both courses are just a short stroll from all the bars and restaurants of the city centre which means that the whole of Chester gets race fever.

H and I love going to the races, well, perhaps I should rephrase that; I love going to the races and H doesn't mind coming with me – sometimes! Whether it's locally at Chester or Haydock, or further afield at Sandown, Epsom or Cheltenham; it makes no difference. There's something about the combination of thoroughbred racehorses, money and the smell of the turf that's intoxicating wherever you go. To have a winner at any of the tracks we visit is fantastic, but to have a winner at your local one is even better.

Six months previously, when I was looking for a horse, I got talking to Chris O'Donnell. Chris used to own a sign manufacturing company and had done quite a bit of work for Eatonfield over the years but his first love has always been racing; in fact I've never met anyone with such an encyclopaedic knowledge of horses and courses as Chris. If you want to know the winner of the Coventry Stakes at

Royal Ascot in 1996 or the runners and riders in the Ayr Gold Cup in 1985 then he's your man. It was Chris who introduced me to bloodstock agent, Bobby O'Ryan.

Chris was with Cheshire trainer, Lisa Williamson when Lisa heard that I was looking for a horse. She saw a particular filly she thought I'd like and 'phoned me straight away.

"She's got potential," she said of three-year-old, Dream of Paradise. "At £5k I think you should buy her, Rob; you won't do better for your money." So I instructed her to buy the filly for me and put her at Lisa's yard in Saighton for training.

Unfortunately, when Dream of Paradise ran at Chester I was in the Bahamas trying to sort out the problems we were having with Jan Ward and Eatonfield's affordable homes development but Lisa told me all about it when I got back.

August 6th was a Sunday and it was a family race day so the Roodee would have been crowded with race goers of all ages soaking up the atmosphere. Lisa told me that Dream of Paradise was running in the 4 o'clock and even though she was an outsider at odds of 25-1 she was adamant that the filly had a chance.

Chris texted me from the track with the news that they were 'off' and I waited in the sun, halfway across the world, until Lisa contacted me with the result.

She told me that as Dream of Paradise raced home the crowd erupted in one big bellow of victory. I wish I'd been there, but it was still an amazing feeling; in fact winning with my own horse at Chester was about as fantastic as scoring a goal for Liverpool, or beating Uncle Frank at cards. It was brilliant! Chris picked up the winner's trophy for me and I couldn't wait to get back to the UK.

The prize money for Dream of Paradise's win was £4k, which is only £1k less than the horse cost in the first place but the money was almost incidental. It was the winning that mattered. I decided I wanted to repeat the feeling as quickly as possible, preferably with a horse that had come from my own yard.

And that's why, in November 2006 after floating on AIM and releasing £5m cash, I started looking for a suitable property for Rob Lloyd Racing.

In mid 2007, Jonathan Major of Chester estate agents, Strutt and Parker, telephoned to inform me that he'd found a property that might be suitable; a 170 acre dairy farm in Spurstow about 18 miles east of Chester. It wasn't on the market yet, but would I like to take a look?

There was something in Jonathan's voice that made me drive over there straight away. He told me to prepare for an unloved and not very pretty collection of farm buildings, but assured me that the location was a good one.

In fact Haycroft Farm is in a fabulous position, but typical of all my personal property purchases it needed a huge amount of money spending on it. The farmhouse needed a total overhaul as did the farm buildings and the land needed a complete new drainage system.

I pulled up in the weed strewn courtyard with H beside me on a lovely sunny morning and the view just took our breath away. We could see for miles over the fields to a distant view of not one castle, but two, with Haycroft Farm forming the apex of a triangle spanning 4,000 years of history.

To the west was the perfectly formed Peckforton Castle, set on the summit of a thickly wooded hill rising sharply from the Cheshire plain. Although the vast medieval-style building appeared to be original it was actually constructed in the mid-19th century by John, 1st Lord Tollemache, who owned huge estates in Cheshire and Suffolk. H and I could see the castle in the distance like a child's drawing, complete with perfectly formed turrets. Then when we turned 40 degrees north we could see the remains of the medieval fortress, Beeston Castle, standing 500ft up on a rocky outcrop. Beeston must have one of the best views of any castle in England – and once again, it looked down on Haycroft.

"It's perfect," I said to H.

"Almost," she added with a smile and she watched me out of the corner of her eye as I started to plan it all out in my mind; the American-style stables I wanted in the derelict barn, the all weather manège, the best horse walkers that money could buy, the spa and solarium and of course, under the shadow of those two castles; the seven furlong all-weather gallops.

"This is going to be Rob Lloyd Racing," I said with more emotion than I'd anticipated and H took my hand as we walked back to the car.

I called Jonathan straight away with a cash offer of £1.85m with no survey and no valuation undertaken. I was worried that if it went on the open market I'd lose it and I knew this was the perfect location for me and for any prospective owners. Haycroft Farm is remote enough to provide a safe environment for the horses but within easy driving distance of Manchester airport and Crewe station for direct trains to London.

My offer was accepted and, from that moment to this, Rob Lloyd Racing has been haemorrhaging cash.

The first big expense was the planning applications which were detailed and complicated to say the least. I needed a quick way to get the planning through the necessary consents as I desperately wanted to be ready for the 2008 flat season to have a hope of recouping any of my investment. I calculated that I would be spending £4m in total and as this was my money, not the bank's, I wanted to be up and running as quickly as possible. I turned to one of our local newspapers, the *Daily Post,* and arranged to speak to David Jones the business correspondent. He interviewed me and gave me the opportunity to make clear what my plans for the development of Haycroft would mean for the area. Ultimately of course, this meant jobs; once the stables was up and running I anticipated 30 jobs would be created.

One of my first appointments was Chris O'Donnell; I asked if he would like to become my racing manager.

I then set up meetings with local residents to inform them of my plans and tried very hard to consider all their views. I was convinced that once everyone could see the finished product I would be home and dry, but of course, I should have known better. In getting Rob Lloyd Racing off the ground I probably made one of the biggest mistakes of my life; I ignored the one thing that as a seasoned property professional you ignore at your peril and one that I would never, ever do as chief executive of Eatonfield plc. I started work on the gallops in the autumn of 2007 before I'd received the necessary consents. I knew I was taking a risk but as far as I was concerned it was a calculated one. Unfortunately what I didn't know at this stage was that the route for the gallops went right across an area known to be occupied by that well-known protected tenant, the Great Crested Newt. It's not as if I hadn't come across him before; I had, plenty of times, but this was my own personal development, I had the horses starting to arrive, a well known trainer, David Murray Smith about to join me and I needed somewhere for the horses to run. I took a chance, started work on the gallops and lived to regret it.

But the biggest regret of all was that Sam was not going to live to see me realise my dream. In late 2007 he took a turn for the worse and it wasn't long before he had to be admitted to hospital. He never came out again; in January 2008 Dad passed away, predeceasing his own mother, Margaret by 12 months.

CHAPTER SIXTEEN

Off the rails

'I went in like a bull in a china shop.'

Sam's death hit me hard. He had been living with me and H at Fron Farm when he died so I saw him every day and watched the gradual deterioration in his health, but it was still a shock. Even though I was married to H, he'd continued to be an influence on me. I remembered how he'd always set me a good example and how he'd demonstrated the importance of staying true to your ambition. Sam had never shirked hard work, regularly putting in 14 hour days and I always admired how he'd built up Flash Farm from nothing. I remember the day he named the herd after the two of us, joining our two names together; Winston and Robert to make Winrob and it was a great feeling, one that I would have liked to repeat in his lifetime. I wished he'd seen me start Rob Lloyd Racing and I wished he could have lived to see the day I would find a horse and name it for him. I realised that so much of what I'd achieved was because of him and I wasn't sure if I'd have that same fire in the belly now that he'd gone.

When it came to the funeral Sam wouldn't have wanted any fuss, but he would have liked everyone to have a good time. All I wanted was for him to go out with a bit of a bang because that way everyone would know just how much he meant to me. Knowing that he would be smiling down at the gesture, I arranged for his coffin to be drawn by four black horses, smart and dignified in their Victorian livery and instead of flowers we had a miniature version of a Spitfire designed in green foliage. Sam was a huge fan of war films and must have seen the *Battle of Britain* at least 100 times. He could recite the whole film word for word and would laugh at the same jokes every time he played the DVD. I even chose a couple of war songs for the service instead of hymns as that seemed much more appropriate.

The church was packed, not just with family, but with friends from all over North Wales and Cheshire as a few days earlier I'd visited all the pubs he used to drink in and dropped off a card with details of the service.

It was a sad day but it was a great day too in many ways. The only person who couldn't come was my grandmother, Margaret. At the age of 97 we felt it would have been too much to expect for her to cope with her own son's death and I'm sure we were right.

One month previously David Murray Smith had travelled from his home in Leicestershire to join us at Haycroft Farm. David had been retired as a trainer for six years after relinquishing his licence in 2001 but I'd persuaded him to pick up the reins again for Rob Lloyd Racing.

When he joined us he was aware of the controversy surrounding our planning application but we all thought the problems would be smoothed over soon enough and in the meantime I told him how grateful I was to have someone of his expertise and track record coming to work for Rob Lloyd Racing. Murray Smith's career spanned more than 30 years in the business and included winners at Cheltenham, Royal Ascot and the Irish Grand National. Prior to joining us he'd trained at Lambourn and Leicester, spent four years with Vincent O'Brien and six with the late, great Major Dick Hern. He trained Rhyme 'n' Reason when he won the Irish Grand National as a novice in 1985; Aquilifer in 1988 when he won the Ritz Club Chase at Cheltenham and Amigo Menor in 1991 when he took the Wokingham at Royal Ascot. As he told a national newspaper at the time: "You have to adapt to the facilities you have. You tweak things, but the principles stay the same. You just have to be open to new ideas."

Murray Smith was certainly open to the idea of how large an operation I wanted Rob Lloyd Racing to be; I told him we were looking at the prospect of 100 horses within two years and I'm pretty sure that's what tempted him out of retirement.

But not everyone was excited about our plans for Rob Lloyd Racing. Thanks to the efforts of a few people in the vicinity of Haycroft Farm more problems were to follow; problems that are still not resolved today.

Not long after Murray Smith arrived the council came down on us like a ton of bricks but rightly or wrongly, I chose to crack on with the renovation work on the outbuildings as well as the installation of the all weather gallops. I was still focused on getting horses on the track for the 2008 season as our costs continued to soar. With any racing stables it's important to have winners and to have winners you've got to have runners in the first place. I upped the stakes and instructed county Kildaire-based Bobby O'Ryan to continue buying for us. Bobby attended sales at Goffs, Tattersalls and Doncaster on our behalf, spending hundreds of thousands of pounds on a number of useful horses over the years, among them Goliath's Boy, Hit the Switch, Broken Applause and Best Bidder, the latter costing us € 150k as a two-year-old.

Bobby bought Broken Applause on my behalf in 2007 before Murray Smith joined us and I chose to put her with trainer Richard Fahey's stables in north Yorkshire. First time out at Haydock she threw jockey Tony Hamilton going down to the starting gates and as I watched from the stands I didn't hold out much hope; this was a five furlong race and she was 11/1 and looked unsettled. But Broken Applause proved me wrong, leaping out of the stalls with complete conviction to settle down mid-division. Then at about halfway, she picked up speed and, with one furlong to go, she edged left and got her nose in front, running on to take the race by one and a half lengths.

This was just as good as Dream of Paradise at Chester

and the celebrations went on long into the night.

Richard Fahey ran Broken Applause in nine more races but she never won again for me, although she did come second in a group three race at Ayr in September 2007. In 2008 I sold her to Tweenhills Stud in Gloucestershire.

Owning a racehorse is a fantastic experience but having your own stables gives you an added buzz because you're much closer to the horses you own. At Haycroft Farm I'm able to watch all my horses as they develop to their full potential, hopefully improving all the time. When you realise just how much hard work it takes to make sure a horse is race fit, then winning that race is even sweeter. I appreciate that our owners at Rob Lloyd Racing want to win and we do everything we can to make that happen but I get almost as big a kick out of watching the horses out on the gallops in the early morning simply because I love horses as much as I love racing. H, however, is not as big a fan but, like all owners, she does enjoy winning.

In 2007 Bobby paid £5.5k for Ocean Glory which we sent to Peter Grayson's stable in Formby. First time out at Warwick and running in the Lloyd Partnership colours of brown and pink he won at 12/1. Lloyd Partnership comprised H, J, Jo and Dan and, according to H, that day in September was the best day she's ever had at the races. She and I watched Ocean Glory pass the finishing post the first of six runners and I don't think she's cheered as loud before or since. The prize money was £3.5k and I then told H we should consider selling him.

"But we can't sell Ocean Glory," said H, completely indignant. "He's our star performer."

Well, since then, he's had six runs, the last one in January 2008 at Kempton, finishing sixth, 10th, 12th and 13th, is still happily resident at Haycroft and has no plans for moving on. If we'd sold him in September 2007 we would probably have realised the optimum price for a horse of his quality.

As soon as David Murray Smith arrived in December we brought most of our horses back to Haycroft Farm, including Ocean Glory. But after just a couple of months at Rob Lloyd Racing it was clear that he and I were going to have a few differences of opinion. We were completely different people with different approaches to life. At 53 Murray Smith is 10 years older than me, a tall, gentlemanly figure who can sometimes appear slightly aloof, whereas I have a tendency to be more direct and when it came to communicating with the staff he didn't always know exactly what was going on in the yard at all times.

Now, I don't mind a bit of youthful high spirits but I do like a sense of discipline, just so long as the horses are happy. There was never any doubt that the horses' well-being was of paramount importance to our new trainer, but I don't think he had his finger on the pulse when it came to discipline and if there's one thing you can't do it's allow discipline in the yard to slip when you're running a £4m operation.

There was one particular incident involving a house I'd rented in the village from one of the local farmers. Because of our planning problems the bed sits I'd planned at Haycroft weren't finished so, as a temporary measure, I was paying for some of the young lads to live in rented accommodation. I heard on the grapevine that they weren't respecting the property; in fact when I visited the house it was dirty and untidy, there were beer bottles everywhere and a door was hanging off its hinges. I was furious and had to send in Ditch and Emily, our racing secretary, to clean the house from top to bottom while Steve Hopwood sorted out the damage.

While all this was going on the council had put an enforcement notice on us, which I appealed against but which you are entitled to work through, until - or if - you receive a stop notice.

A stop notice duly followed and then we really did have to down tools; there was nothing else we could do and all building work at Haycroft Farm ceased immediately. But even with our unresolved and ongoing problems we decided to continue with plans for the official open day. By now we had 38 horses stabled at Haycroft Farm and a top-notch five star establishment. We had the best of everything; just as I'd envisaged when H and I first came to view the dilapidated buildings and weed-strewn courtyard less than 12 months ago. We'd achieved a huge amount and I was extremely proud of what Rob Lloyd Racing stood for but, as a result, I was financially and emotionally drained.

CHAPTER SEVENTEEN

Contentious objectors

'We had no trainer for a total of five months and I had to make some very difficult decisions.'

Jason pulled out all the stops and arranged a brilliant open day on 6th April 2008 which was made slightly more difficult by a heavy fall of snow the previous night. We anticipated about 200 people coming to see us; local residents, friends and family with some future clients thrown in for good measure. The day was scheduled to start at 11am with Rob Lloyd Racing to be declared officially open by Mike Cattermole of Channel 4 racing. We calculated that the day would finish around 2 o'clock.

In the end J reckoned we had more than 500 visitors through the gates and goodness knows when the final car pulled out of the car park. By the time the last visitor waved goodbye, the champagne and nibbles had long gone, the grass in the fields was completely churned up and the debris dotted around the stables looked a little forlorn, but the residents of Spurstow, on the whole, had come to shake my hand. I think they could see that my heart was in the right place and that, when it came down to it, Rob Lloyd Racing would be a positive influence on the area.

However, with every development I've ever worked on there have always been one or two niggles from objectors and this one was no exception. Comments were made about the colour of the barn roof and an objection was lodged by three people in the village regarding the planned addition of a heli-pad that later made the front page of the *Chester Chronicle*. Fortunately, it didn't stop some new owners approaching us with enquiries and J and I considered that, overall, Rob Lloyd Racing's open day had been a great success.

We continued with the renovations where we could; we put in 50 bird and three owl boxes, we landscaped areas of the site following some residents' requests, we put in an orchard and a vineyard, in fact we pulled out all the stops but we were still having problems with the gallops and now we had the added problem with the heli-pad, which in my opinion, had the potential to be just as damaging. If Rob Lloyd Racing was going to be the best then it had to be seen to have the best of everything and that included a facility for owners to fly in, see their horses and fly out again.

The three objectors appeared to have one particular lady at the forefront of the campaign, in fact she continues to create an obstruction for us today and I can see no logical explanation for what she's doing. It's not as if we don't have helicopters flying over the area anyway: Haycroft Farm is on the flight path to Manchester airport, there's a fuel pipeline running right across our land and there's a helicopter that regularly flies the line. Yet she continues to object to a heli-pad. I have invited her to Haycroft to show her around, explain what we're doing and discuss our plans for the future but she simply refuses to meet me, preferring to talk about me behind my back instead.

After the open day, another resident of Spurstow, Kevin Thompson, telephoned to say that he was concerned about the position of a barn we were planning to build at Haycroft. I met Kevin to discuss his objections and then agreed to move the barn so it wouldn't obscure his view. The solution was arrived at amicably, in a responsible fashion after consultation between us and I can't understand why this shouldn't also be the case with the heli-pad objector. Even her immediate neighbours are puzzled by her refusal to entertain the idea.

While all this was going on I was still trying desperately hard to placate the council and eventually approached them in person to explain why I'd started work before the planning was approved. I was at that time employing 20 staff and now had owners coming into the yard but nowhere to take them for a cup of coffee or a bacon sandwich. Not only did I need the gallops for the horses, I needed to convert the outbuildings into offices and a comfortable lounge. I admitted to the council that I had done it all too quickly. I held up my hands and said: "I've made a mistake and I'm sorry" and hoped they would take a more flexible approach. As I said to H; if I had my time again, I would do it all very differently. I would start Rob Lloyd Racing much more slowly and build the business gradually; just a few horses at first in a small yard, then I would expand at a sensible pace. This time, I did wonder if I'd raised the bar too high. But there was no going back now. I was committed and I couldn't give up; I just had to pray that the council would be lenient.

Crewe and Nantwich Borough Council refused to budge. I told David Murray Smith about the stop notice and I also told him that I now had to consider sending most of our horses to other trainers. Not only would this be bad for morale in the yard, it was also inconvenient and incredibly expensive. If I chose this option I would be considerably out of pocket. It also wouldn't help the already strained relationship between Murray Smith and the rest of the yard.

The added problem, as if I needed another, was that the bottom was just about to fall out of the property market. It wasn't just the planning issues that were causing problems now, it was the economy too; any potential owners who may have considered putting a racehorse with me where now deciding that they couldn't afford to take the risk.

All in all 2008 was a disastrous year. We didn't have the proper facilities as the gallops weren't ready, we had injuries and sickness and the situation at the stables ended up going from bad to worse.

In April and May a lot of the horses were coughing so I accepted that things were a little slow, but as long as the future of Rob Lloyd Racing looked rosy I could take the rough with the smooth and our trainer did acknowledge to the press that we had a number of useful two-year-olds coming up. If David Murray Smith was positive about our future then others would be bound to listen. The racing world is an incestuous one and you have to be careful what you say. Too much bad news and prospective owners can be scared off.

Unfortunately, it seemed as if Murray Smith kept all the bad news for my ears alone. I used to love coming down to the stables, spending all day Saturday and Sunday getting stuck in, enjoying the fact that I didn't have to think of Eatonfield plc but could just concentrate on my horses instead. But now, my trainer was ready for me with news that one of the horses had just gone lame, that one had a snotty nose or another had ringworm. In the end, I dreaded weekends and whatever sad tale of woe was coming next.

Then, would you believe it, almost against the odds, we had our first winner in June. Five-year-old Piper's Song ran at Beverley in the 3.45pm 1m 2f handicap, coming late under jockey Pat Cosgrave to beat Princess Cocoa by half a length.

Murray Smith's achievement was nominated as the star performance of the day by the *Racing Post* and it was obvious that a lot of people in the racing world were very happy that he'd made a comeback, none more so than me.

This was a man who had achieved a lot in his career and I could see that he was relishing the new challenge after seven years on the sidelines.

But of course, even the best trainer in the world can't train his horses without a gallops and I was forced to take the decision to transport our horses to Broxton, six miles away, as a temporary measure. This meant the yard staff loading and unloading the horses, ferrying them backwards and forwards to a gallops that we were now having to pay to use by the hour. I knew I was just putting off the inevitable; sooner or later I would have to make the decision to move most of the horses to other trainers.

In July I was interviewed by the *Flintshire Chronicle* and I made it clear that if we couldn't get necessary planning for the gallops I was considering moving Rob Lloyd Racing lock, stock and barrel to another location.

My frustration also showed in another interview when I expressed my disappointment that some local residents who had enjoyed my hospitality at the open day were now objecting to our horses using the gallops at all. The situation had escalated and suddenly it wasn't just newts we had to contend with; some people wanted us out of Spurstow altogether. I explained that we had 40 horses, two of which were already entered for the Goffs Million. I also stated that there was a distinct possibility that we might have to close completely with the loss of 21 jobs. Journalist Rolf Johnson described it perfectly: *'Newts and nimbies had derailed me.'*

During this time, it's fair to say that Murray Smith and I weren't agreeing on too many things. One of our disagreements concerned the way he dealt with any physical problems we had with the horses. I'm a firm believer in 'working through' an injury, if it's a minor one of course, whereas Murray Smith was keen to keep the horse in the stable and call the vet, often unnecessarily in my opinion.

But the biggest problem was the lack of communication. After the trainer the most important position in the yard is the head girl or boy, and there has to be a connection between them; it's the only way a trainer can find out what's going on with the horses on a day-to-day basis. Unfortunately Murray Smith and Becky, my head girl, didn't have a particularly close relationship, so Becky just had to get on with her job the best she could with minimal feedback.

After six months with Rob Lloyd Racing, Murray Smith tendered his resignation and I accepted it. I genuinely wish him well and I'm very sorry it didn't work out for us and, of course, I sympathise with the fact that he now has to find another job.

At this stage Rob Lloyd Racing had 40 horses and no trainer; in fact we had no trainer for a total of five months and I had to make some very difficult decisions.

CHAPTER EIGHTEEN

We win some; we lose some

'Owning and running a racing yard could be the one time in my life when I have to admit I've allowed my heart to rule my head.'

I have made no secret of the fact that running a racing stables in its initial stages is one of the best ways to spend money as if it's going out of fashion, but part of the reason for this was because I insisted on having the best of everything. The barn had been transformed into a top notch stables with capacity for 50 horses, we had two of the best horse walkers on the market, a manège, a spa and a solarium. But we also had the added expense of paying for all the horses we'd moved to other trainers. It was a disastrous situation and one that I couldn't see being resolved in the near future.

I decided to put 17 of our two-year-olds with Richard Fahey in Malton north Yorks; 12 horses with Lisa Williamson just up the road in Saighton and one with Brendan Powell in Lambourn. There were a few horses still left at Rob Lloyd Racing and we kept them ticking over with regular walks but it was a very difficult time and I had to make a lot of redundancies. Amazingly we lost only one owner. Because of my decision to move the horses the overheads went through the roof but I had no choice; we had 29 two-year-olds at the time and they had to run or you couldn't get any value for them. It was a Catch-22 situation.

However, it wasn't all doom and gloom; we did have some runners, including two horses in the Goffs Million, the richest juvenile race in the racing calendar. Anfield Star, who was with Ger Lyons at the time, ran in Rob Lloyd Racing's colours in the 2.55pm colt's race, finishing a disappointing 18 of 19 runners while Best Bidder, who was with Richard Fahey, came 15th of 24 in the fillies' race. We even had some winners. We had eight winners in the 2008 season which, from a disastrous start, was a big recovery.

I was there in October 2008 when Goliath's Boy won a 7f maiden race at Catterick and watched as Dan proudly lifted the trophy for us in the winner's enclosure. The horse had quite a bit of class finishing fourth in a French listed race at Saint-Cloud later that year, after which Richard Fahey asked if I wanted to sell him. I resisted at first but eventually agreed and in January 2009 Goliath's Boy left Haycroft Farm; a sad day for me and one I will never forget, given the circumstances in which the horse left.

As most people keep reminding me: I never give up. I kept plugging away with positive PR as well as the practicalities with the council. Finally on 15th August 2008 we were granted planning permission for our all-weather gallops but with stipulations attached relating to the flora and fauna. Cheers went up around the yard and I took a deep breath and agreed to all the conditions. Rob Lloyd Racing was finally up and running. Now all I had to deal with were one or two remaining staffing problems in the yard.

Strange as it may seem there was one advantage to all the problems we'd experienced during those difficult months. After all the upheaval at Rob Lloyd Racing; the transporting of horses, paying fees to other trainers, losing Murray Smith, the protracted problems with planning and all the redundancies I had to make, I did succeed in sorting out the wheat from the chaff when it came to staffing. It's always been difficult to find good quality employees in the world of racing and we all have to recruit from overseas - we have a couple of lads from India at the moment, for example. This can result in staff having difficulty settling in and us having problems following up references. I've read CVs that state the applicant is a 'rider of the highest standard' and then we put them on a horse and it's plain to see that they can barely ride at all. You can't afford to take a chance that the person sitting in the saddle isn't competent; these thoroughbred horses cost thousands of pounds, sometimes hundreds of thousands of pounds and they need careful handling. So when it came to getting our staffing levels back up again Becky and I made sure we recruited very carefully indeed. Fortunately, some of the staff we'd let go went on to find alternative employment at establishments close by.

By Christmas 2008 we'd managed to get all the horses back in their stables at Haycroft Farm and on January 1st I recruited another trainer, Pat Morris, who was spotted by Bobby O'Ryan our bloodstock manager in Ireland. Pat came from the Curragh and it is with a huge sigh of relief that I say there is hope now; there is light at the end of the tunnel. More importantly, there is discipline in the yard.

With the benefit of hindsight and if I had to do it all again I would do it differently next time. Owning and running a racing yard could be the one time in my life when I have to admit I've allowed my heart to rule my head. My ambition was to have one of the biggest yards outside Newmarket and I believe that my ambition can still be achieved, but I should have done it much more gradually.

Even so, in this part of Cheshire, I'm in good company and there are one or two others who are either mad enough or committed enough to have done the same. Donald McCain, Ginger's son, is just down the road at Cholmondeley and 11 miles away in Malpas, Michael Owen runs Manor House Stables. Michael's establishment was up and running a year before Rob Lloyd Racing and he seems to have kept an eye on our progress.

Manor House Stables and Haycroft Farm have more similarities than differences; we've both got five star facilities and we're both working hard to attract owners but

I think Michael and his trainer, Nicky Vaughan, doubted we would succeed in achieving what we set out to do, probably because they know first hand how difficult it is. They've got about 40 horses themselves and they know exactly how much it costs to run a stables – about three quarters of a million pounds a year at the last count - and they know how hard it is to get an operation like ours off the ground. What is interesting is that I've noticed his PR firm keeping an eye on the number of column inches Rob Lloyd Racing has in the local papers, often issuing a statement of their own soon afterwards.

Ironically, after our slow start, the biggest problem Rob Lloyd Racing has to contend with now is keeping up with our programme of development. Since Pat Morris joined us we're getting calls almost daily from prospective owners and we need more space. Some of our current owners, such as my old friend and one time adversary, Mac have been with us since the beginning. Others, like businessman, Michael Green, joined us 12 months ago.

In August last year Michael and I were at the Roodee together. Michael is a keen race goer and I'd been trying to persuade him to become an owner with Rob Lloyd Racing for a while since I knew that he'd been considering making the commitment. Michael and I had had a disappointing day with no winners and then in the last I spotted a horse by Invincible Spirit that I fancied the look of.

I remembered Invincible Spirit winning the six furlong group one Stanley Leisure Sprint Cup at Haydock in 2002 beating favourite Malhub by a short head. With a pedigree like that surely this horse had a chance today and we might be able to claw back some of the cash we'd lost?

"Let's put 50 quid each on the nose," I said, daring Michael to up his stake.

"Bit more than I'm used to," laughed Michael, but he rose to the challenge and whipped out his wallet.

Suffice to say, the horse won easily; the excitement of the win easing the pain of our five previous unplaced runners.

As we were celebrating, Bobby O'Ryan called me on my mobile from the breeze-up sales. Earlier on in the day I'd turned down a couple of the horses Bobby had offered me as they were over budget but when he told me he'd just seen a two-year-old in the ring by Invincible Spirit my ears pricked up. The timing was just too good to be true.

I handed the 'phone to Michael and listened as he told Bobby he was interested in this particular colt; the coincidence of having just won on another horse by Invincible Spirit had made an impression on him too. Bobby bought the colt on our instructions and arranged for it to be brought over to Haycroft Farm. Michael named his horse Green Spirit and it's the first horse he's ever owned.

After a disappointing season last year, with injuries keeping him away from the track, we're all looking forward to seeing Green Spirit as a three-year-old. He's a good horse and one that trainer, Pat Morris, says looks effortless on the gallops. Let's hope he can replicate that speed and style on the track. He'll be running at Doncaster, getting a feel for the occasion and then we'll get him ready for Chester in May. I cannot imagine the excitement if the horse wins; Michael will go wild! Rest assured that Pat will do his absolute best to make that happen.

I really admire the way Pat looks after all the horses here at Haycroft; we're working well together and it's a great buzz. Pat didn't have particularly good horses in Ireland when he was working at the Curragh as a public trainer but he was winning with them and here he's got a brilliant chance of repeating his form. There have been one or two lingering problems with staff on the yard but he's got the right attitude; he makes sure I know exactly what's going on and that's very important to me.

There was one particular incident that illustrates Pat's attitude perfectly and involved H's horse, Honey Berry. The yard boy had let the horse off the walker when the horse was spooked for some reason. The lad turned around and hit Honey Berry, just missing her eye. If there's one thing I can't stand it's cruelty towards the horses and if I'd been there on the yard that day or, even worse, seen it happen I would have strung the lad up by his boots.

When Pat told me what had happened I wiped the floor with the lad in front of Pat and Becky and told him to keep out of my way for the next few days. But when I thought about the incident later, I knew in my heart that I had to let him go; I just didn't trust him any more.

It's good to know that Pat and I also see eye-to-eye on vets: neither of us are big fans, although Nantwich

Veterinary Group, the practice we use, is one of the best in the country in my opinion. They understand the horses here at Haycroft; they're not just in the business to make money and we have a strong relationship with Alasdair Topp, the practice's racing horse specialist. Alasdair is also the racecourse vet for Haydock, Aintree and Uttoxeter so he knows exactly what he's talking about. I'm also impressed with D E Evans in Mold, the vets we use for Cloverdale Bloodstock.

However, when Sam had Flash Farm we wouldn't call the vet unless there was something seriously wrong with the herd, such as milk fever. Farmers and livestock people often know more about their animals than vets do and at Haycroft we don't always believe that it's a good idea to go down the drugs route, administering antibiotics at the drop of a hat. If a horse has a cold, Pat will give it honey or garlic rather than giving it an injection and we let the infection work through the horse's system naturally. Pat is also a dab hand at massaging a horse's problems away, stiffness in the joints seem to disappear under his magic touch.

Today, if you were to ask me if I have any regrets regarding Rob Lloyd Racing, then no, not now, but a year ago it would have been a completely different story. As I said to H: What I should have done is got the yard up and running first, completed the gallops, bought five or six horses of my own, employed a trainer, and built up the owners. What I've done instead is go at it like a bull in a china shop – which is the way I tend to approach a lot of things. It's like in business: no deal is too big. And it's also just like learning to ride at Lodge Farm; if I fall off, I just get straight back on again. With Eatonfield there's always been a way to get funding; there's always been a way to bring in a partner and do a deal. All I can say in my defence with Rob Lloyd Racing is that I'm still learning in this business, but more determined than ever to get there.

CHAPTER NINETEEN

Staff changes and company expansion

'I'll admit I was finding it a strain to comply with the restrictions imposed on me now that I was the chief executive of a plc, but asking my chauffeur to spy on me was ridiculous.'

Helen has often asked me why Rob Lloyd Racing concentrates on training racehorses for the flat rather than for the National Hunt since my other stated ambition has always been to train a Grand National winner. In 2007 we already had some horses capable of going over jumps; Piper's Song, Rob Lloyd Racing's first winner, likes to jump as does Sandy's Legend, in fact Sandy won at Uttoxeter over the hurdles in November 2008. But because of the size of the fences and the length of the race you need a very special horse for the Grand National; it is after all the hardest race in the world.

At Rob Lloyd Racing we're constantly looking for that horse; a horse that we might see at a point-to-point for example, one that's got the ability to jump big fences and one that's got staying power. It might only be a five or six-year-old at the moment but we'll know if it's got the potential to go further. Owners like jumpers; it's as simple as that. Donald McCain in Cholmondeley has more than 100 horses most trained over the jumps and when I think of Donald, I automatically think of his father, Ginger McCain, Red Rum's trainer. When I think of Red Rum I naturally think of Nan West and winning my first bet in 1973. So you see; I'll never give up the dream of training a Grand National winner, because I'm constantly reminded of it.

It had been a frantic 18 months for Rob Lloyd Racing between buying Haycroft farm in 2007 to recruiting trainer Pat Morris in January 2009 but I was also working hard at building the bloodstock side of my business. Since 2005, Cloverdale had done well for me but, worldwide, the bloodstock business has taken quite a few knocks.

Until recently bloodstock was a profitable business to be in, but 2008 was a difficult one for everyone in the racing world. Racehorses and power boats are always the first luxuries to suffer in a recession and this one is proving to be no different.

The yearling sales begin in France in August, finishing in the UK in December. At the end of 2008, some reports in the industry stated that yearling prices had fallen by up to 50% in some countries – with the USA top of the list. Fortunately, we were managing to keep our head above water, but only just.

When we first started in the bloodstock business we

spent about £5k to £12k per foal, but since then we've increased the quality year on year; we've raised the bar in fact. In November 2008 Bobby O'Ryan bought seven foals for Cloverdale at Goffs in Ireland at a cost of £200k, but I don't know what the market will be like when we come to put them through the ring, all I can say is that every one of the foals has a good pedigree.

Most trainers in the business don't actually own the horses in their yard. Instead, he or she will be given an order stating a price of, say, £20k or £100k and the trainer will buy a horse of that value on the owner's behalf. Alternatively, a trainer may use a bloodstock agent to do the buying for them in the way that we do at Rob Lloyd Racing.

Very few trainers that I know of also have a bloodstock side to their business and I don't know anyone who's also chief executive of a public limited company.

In 2007/8 Eatonfield plc had a very good year; profits increased for the last six months to £5.81m before tax, up 48% from £3.43m in 2006/7 with operating profit up 43% to £5.14m compared to £3.6m in the previous year. Eatonfield was doing well and I was happy with our current position. Unfortunately, there was a certain amount of unhappiness amongst the staff which was totally unrelated to the success we were enjoying as a company.

Terry Carroll joined Eatonfield as Financial Director in 2006 and was instrumental in helping us get through the AIM float. He graduated from Bradford Business School in

1970 before qualifying as a chartered accountant and since then had held positions as Treasurer of Halifax Building Society, Chief Executive of National & Provincial Building Society and Chief Exec or FD of a number of other unquoted businesses. More importantly, he had already had experience of privatisation and flotation projects and had been involved with a number of mergers and acquisitions. Carroll's credentials were ideal and he made his presence felt fairly quickly at the head office in Mold. Unfortunately, it became clear to me in our board meetings that not everybody warmed to him.

Legal Director Keith Mather had always chaired our board meetings in the past but Carroll now assumed responsibility. Following the transition from private to public company he saw the role of FD as a much more important one and he wasn't shy in communicating that to the others in the office. He succeeded in upsetting not just Keith but Jan, my PA and even H who said Carroll had an unfortunate way with words that left her feeling interrogated when he spoke to her. Things reached such a head that Phil Middlehurst, our Accounts Controller, resigned saying he could no longer work with him.

Throughout his 12 months at Eatonfield I never doubted that Terry Carroll was competent at his job, the problem was; I don't think he just wanted to be Financial Director, I'm sure he wanted to be Chief Executive: He wanted my job! I would have had no problem with that fact if he was capable of doing the deals, but all the evidence pointed to the contrary, which was why the time he spent with us was so fraught. There's no denying that Carroll was instrumental in guiding us through the float but it was a big price to pay for his attitude towards his colleagues, an attitude which I also struggled with at times. If he and I had meetings in London, for example, I didn't look forward to having dinner with him at the end of the day simply because he would go on and on and on about the magazine articles and books he'd written; a harmless habit, I suppose, but it was irritating. Deep down I suspected that he was just a lonely man who found small talk difficult, but what I couldn't ignore was the strange situation with Ditch and the diary.

It all started with a comment that Carroll made to Ditch when I was out of earshot.

"Paul, I'd like you to start keeping a diary of your whereabouts when you're out and about with Rob."

"A what?" asked Ditch.

"A diary; you know, a record of exactly where you go – every day."

Ditch told me this interesting snippet of information a couple of months later, after he'd already come up with a few excuses to stall Carroll and was now running out of ideas. Ditch said to me that he didn't feel he could come up with a believable excuse for a fourth time in a row.

Naturally, I wasn't happy with the idea of my Financial Director going behind my back. I'll admit I was finding it a strain to comply with the restrictions imposed on me now that I was the chief executive of a plc, but asking my chauffeur to spy on me was ridiculous.

At the next board meeting Carroll, Suki Kalirai and Sir Leslie insisted that I make Ditch redundant. His salary had now become an expense that they felt the company could no longer afford.

I dreaded giving Ditch the bad news but he was fairly cool about the whole thing.

"Don't worry about it, Rob," he said. "I was gutted when I was made redundant after 20 years at United Utilities; nothing could ever be as bad as that. I managed to get a job once; I'm pretty sure I can do it again."

And that's when I made the decision to switch Ditch to Rob Lloyd Racing and put him on my personal payroll.

Two months later, on 12th September 2007 Terry Carroll resigned and Howard Jones, his deputy, became the new FD at Eatonfield plc. I then re-employed Phil Middlehurst on a part-time basis for Rob Lloyd Racing and at the same time began to wonder about the quality of the staff I was employing elsewhere in the company.

Eatonfield now had three satellite offices based in Cardiff, Newcastle and Bristol, each one with its own land buyer on the lookout for suitable developments around the UK but I wasn't convinced that our investment in these new offices with all the overheads they incurred was actually worth it. As an employer, it's difficult to find the right people with the necessary mentality to act as land buyers. Anyone can buy land; it's buying at the right price and adding value that's important. I have found over the years that there are a lot of people who will happily take the wage but don't have the motivation to go the extra distance. I wanted to surround myself with the likes of Steve Hopwood and Moi Jones, our landscape gardener; quality professionals like Keith Mather and Phil Middlehurst, Steve Jones and Ian Arnott, all of whom I could trust and were loyal to a fault. We've always paid good salaries at Eatonfield and I reward hard work, but by the same token it's important when running a business to weed out those who don't pull their weight.

A good example of the occasional irresponsible attitude to cash was the Langley House development in Wilmslow. This was the dilapidated property in seven acres that we bought in 2006 with three smaller properties in the grounds. We eventually lost £1.5m on that development which, as I've said, was ridiculous. Even though we sold the original house straight away for £1m, thereby covering the costs of buying the whole development, we didn't keep a close enough eye on the finances when we renovated the other three properties in the grounds. I was left extremely disappointed by the way that project was run.

Since the Langley House development we've cut back dramatically on residential, eventually freezing all house building by mid 2008 and reducing the staff in Eatonfield Developments to just a core team. Financially, Langley House simply wasn't tightly controlled enough and we learnt our lesson or - shall I say - I learnt mine.

In 2007 it wasn't clear yet if any of my children were

keen to follow in my footsteps. At the beginning of the year J was at Reading University studying international banking and finance, Jo was studying for her 'A' levels and Dan was in his final year at Rydal.

Yet just nine months later J announced that he wanted to leave university and get started in the real world. I couldn't argue with him; I remembered how keen I was to earn my first pay cheque, so I didn't stand in his way.

At the beginning of 2008 J started up his own company, The Waterstown Club; a unique horseracing club which allows all members the opportunity to follow a racehorse for 12 months both in training and on the track.

He also accompanied me on visits to institutions in the city, learning the pitfalls and picking up tips. I won't deny that I can open doors for him, but he has to make the most of his opportunities and I'm enjoying watching him do just that. He wants to build a diverse group of companies and he's looking at all sorts of ideas at the moment. If he gets it right and with a bit of guidance from me he could be 15 years ahead of the game because I can teach him the street fighting aspect of running a company. J's got the business brain; he just needs the brawn to go with it. I have no doubt that by the time he's 25 J will be a millionaire.

In 2007 Jo was studying hard for her 'A' levels at Gordonstoun and keen to take a gap year afterwards. She had plans to travel round Australia and New Zealand and after that she wasn't sure what she wanted to do. Again, I get the feeling that Jo would like to run her own business;

whether she wishes to work with me is another matter.

Dan was still at Rydal, enjoying his rugby and taking an active part in the drama club. If I had to make a prediction I'd say that Dan's future lay in the city as a top lawyer or accountant, his intelligence and attention to detail would make him perfect for just such a career. On the other hand, he may consider taking his interest in drama a step further; I have it on very good authority he's a talented performer.

One thing's for sure; my children are all different from each other and they're quite different to me but if there's one thing we all share it's our love of horses. All three of them love going to the races and J, in particular, will get out on the gallops at Haycroft on a Saturday morning while I have a chat with Pat about the horses in the yard. It's great knowing I have such well adjusted kids, even better when you know you can rely on them when the going gets tough and during 2008 the going was going to get very tough indeed.

CHAPTER TWENTY

The timing isn't right

'This was a market that no-one had experienced before and one that I knew Eatonfield could make money in.'

At the beginning of 2008 the future was full of possibilities for Eatonfield. We had a new FD in Howard Jones and a desire to build on our successes as well as put into practice any lessons we'd learnt from our mistakes. One of the secrets of a successful business is to hold your hands up when you've made a mistake and prove you can learn from it, which was just what I was about to do with an 83 acre secluded site in Lanarkshire, 20 miles south of Glasgow.

Birkwood in Lesmahagow was owned by the NHS and was a large Grade B listed property, unoccupied since 2002. It was bigger but not dissimilar to the Langley House development that we lost money on in 2006 and I was determined not to make the same mistake again. We were introduced to the site as an off-market opportunity and in June 2008 we completed on the purchase. Steve Jones, Eatonfield's Director of Planning, subsequently prepared an application for 130 residential units with the proposal that the main building be converted into an hotel, complete with leisure facilities.

The size of the Birkwood development also showed, following the Corus site in Workington, that the average size of our developments was increasing. It was obvious to anyone following Eatonfield's progress that we could apply our skills just as well to the bigger sites as the smaller ones. Langley House had seven acres; Birkwood was 12 times bigger.

I'm pleased to say that the planning application has had widespread support from local residents and if the plans go through, hopefully within the next few months, we will be looking for an appropriate hotel organisation to join us in developing the site.

In August 2008 I was keen for Eatonfield to expand further and our brokers Evolution Securities Ltd stated that this wouldn't be a problem even though the property market was looking a little uncertain. Andrew Umbers, Executive Director at Evolution, was convinced that raising £15m was a possibility which meant that if I wanted to keep my 48% stake in the company I would have to put up about £7m of my own money; money that I didn't have at the time. If I didn't subscribe then my share in Eatonfield would be diluted.

All the other main shareholders; SAAD, UBS and GAM were all interested in subscribing but hadn't committed.

I then got a call from Andrew Umbers telling me that he

thought Evolution could comfortably raise between £50m and £100m for us since Eatonfield Group plc had moved up a level and he was getting very good feedback from the institutions. He also stated that the opportunity was there for me to take more cash out of the business.

I decided that the time was right and we started work straight away on a three week road show, intending to present to about 37 investors. Then with supremely bad timing I opened the *Financial Times* on the very first day of the road show and read an article stating an investment company had lost approximately £700m in its share value in one day.

Every single day after that the news was the same, with the word 'recession' flashing like a red beacon in the financial pages of all the newspapers. Comments such as "You're going too early" and "The market's going to get worse" killed Evolution's plans dead in the water and of course we didn't get it away. Our share price went down from 130p to 115p to 100p to 90p, ending at 88p. I would have still run at 88p, but it wasn't to be. Today's share price (March 09) stands at about 5p.

The only consolation I have is that every other property developer I know is in the same boat. Sometimes it needs an uncertain market to realise what your strengths and weaknesses are as a developer. Fortunately for us we had come out of the investment market about three years previously to concentrate on our brownfield developments. We weren't as vulnerable as some other property companies I knew.

In 2008 the residential side of Eatonfield was completely static. In the early days of developing sustainable homes there were some buyers who would specifically request these types of properties, but as soon as the downturn in the residential market took hold Eatonfield suffered badly; not only do eco homes cost more to build, but the lack of available buyers meant we lost out twice, which was great for the customer keen to negotiate a good deal, but not so great for Eatonfield.

Towards the end of 2007 we'd already significantly reduced the number of new builds in development as sales had almost come to a standstill. The lack of mortgages for buyers meant that prices for new homes had to go lower which also meant lower year end asset values. We had a residential land bank spread over a number of sites, primarily in Wales, with existing planning permission for 530 plots and a further 1,287 potential plots going through planning and we knew we could choose to develop these sites when the market improved or sell them off as oven-ready sites to one of the larger residential house builders. In the meantime overdraft facilities were agreed through to September 2009 with our two main bankers.

In March 2008 Eatonfield plc reported an increase in profit to £2.29m, six months later we reported a fall in profits of 12%, although the £4m pre-tax profit was still a respectable one given the condition of the property market at the time. I knew that we had to adapt to a very different market place from the one we had at the time of our 2007 review and I knew that one way to do this was to continue to explore joint ventures and profit share agreements as a lower risk way of gaining entry to new projects. Our intention was to conserve working capital until the market settled, reduce the number of sites and speculative builds and sell some undeveloped sites. The contrast with 2007 was stark, when we had exceeded market expectations but then as I said before; everyone was in the same boat.

In October 2008 H and I were on a much needed break but within hours of leaving, my mobile 'phone was ringing.

"Leave it," said H, desperate to distract me but as I glanced down I could see Howard Jones' name on screen. I'd chatted to our FD only yesterday, telling him that H and I were going away for a few days. It must be urgent, so I took the call.

Howard explained the severity of our financial situation and my expression must have said it all because H guessed that the situation was serious.

"Not again, Rob. Do we ever get a break from the business?"

Eatonfield needed investment and it needed it fast. The first port of call was the shareholders but none of the other shareholders were prepared to offer further investment as they were too busy preserving cash themselves. Added to that, the word 'property' was now a dirty word in the City. So I stepped into the breach and offered a loan of £750k from Rob Lloyd Racing which I was willing to propose as a short term solution along with an increased personal guarantee of the group's debt to £1m. For the loan of £750k I proposed that I be entitled to a 50% profit share on both the Corus and Birkwood sites.

Fortunately the resolutions relating to both the loan and profit share were passed unanimously. As Howard explained, even though Eatonfield had borrowings of £33.5m against assets of £53m we had been unable to raise further finance against the value of the former Corus site in Workington which meant there was less cash available than expected. The remaining two board members; Sir Leslie and Suki Kalirai, both believed that the injection of cash would take us through to the point where the Corus site could be refinanced with the benefit of planning permission.

In the meantime we sold a parcel of land at Greenfield, Holywell in North Wales for £2m, raising £520k after repayment of debt.

I knew that 2008 had been a challenging year so far and that valuations had fallen a long way from the peak of 2007 but the outlook wasn't completely bleak; looking at the situation from another angle, the downturn was bound to bring opportunities for Eatonfield regarding off-market distressed purchases. But I was under no illusions about the residential housing market and didn't see an upturn in that sector for at least two years.

Following Eatonfield's injection of cash I now had to give some serious thought as to what to do next. I knew there were some difficult decisions to be made in order to for us to keep trading, the first of which was to reduce our overheads by a planned £500k a year.

We took the decision to close our satellite offices in Bristol, Cardiff and Newcastle as well as moving out of our head office in Mold, making the latter available for lease or sale. We moved most of the staff into available space at Haycroft Farm which resulted in unavoidable redundancies along the way but meant my life was made a little easier as I now had both businesses under one roof. We put a stop to speculative new house building and unconditional land acquisitions and we reappraised planning consents on existing sites to improve land values.

Our FD, Howard Jones, did a fantastic job handling the redundancies for Eatonfield and I will always be grateful for his professional and sympathetic approach to the staff affected. It's never easy telling people that their job no longer exists but in this case, we really had no choice.

In light of all the above, a £4m pre-tax profit was very respectable indeed, albeit one largely based on revaluation of two of our key investment properties; Corus and Birkwood. Our profit after tax was £2.8m with no dividend proposed. On 10th November 2008 Howard resigned with the offer of a job in Scotland, one which he'd been considering for some time. Until another financial director was appointed, Phil Middlehurst stepped into the breach.

To my mind the property market in 2008 was now worse than any other in living memory and many of my colleagues' businesses were really feeling the pinch. At the end of the year I had a breakfast meeting with one of the directors of a commercial property consultants in Liverpool. He told me that this time last year he was worth around £50m; today he'd be lucky to scrape £5m together. The evidence to prove this sort of statement was everywhere you looked. In January 2009, a report published by IPD the leading index provider stated that commercial property values fell by 27.1% in 2008, decimated by the reduced availability of credit and the falling demand for new space.

As Brendan Flood, my good friend and MD of Modus, said: "We're not in expansion mode now, we're in preservation mode."

Visiting the institutions in London at the beginning of 2009, it was obvious the situation was desperate and there were a number of people still threatening to jump off balconies. Eatonfield had managed to come out of the situation relatively safely by keeping the banks informed and keeping them on our side. I believed that it wouldn't be long before we touched the bottom of the market and it was important that Eatonfield made the most of any opportunities that came our way once we were down there. This was a market that no-one had experienced before and one that I knew Eatonfield could make money in but I also knew that I had to be patient. Given my desire to dive in and do the bigger deal it wasn't easy for me to take the foot off the gas, but of course I had to; the secret was knowing when to accelerate again. It was while I was waiting for that moment to arrive that I received a call from Jamie Steel of RDF Media.

"What would you think if we offered you the opportunity to be the subject of one of the episodes of the next series of *Secret Millionaire?*" he asked.

"I'd rather you didn't do it," said H when I mentioned the 'phone call to her that night and I probably would have agreed with her wishes if I'd received the call in 2007 or 2009, but this was 2008 and while I was busy, I felt there was a window of opportunity to squeeze something else into my life. I'd wanted to raise the bar on my charity work for some time and this was my chance to do it.

CHAPTER TWENTY ONE

Who wants to be a Secret Millionaire?

'I'd feel guilty if I didn't work this hard. I've been given a lot of opportunities in my life; I feel that I have to make the most of them.'

"I can think of plenty of reasons why you shouldn't do *Secret Millionaire*," said H as she stood in the kitchen at Fron Farm in August 2008.

"Really? And what are they?" I asked, genuinely interested in what H had to say.

"Well for a start, you haven't got the time and more importantly, you don't know just how much TV will pry into your life. There might be some bitter ex-colleague from your past, just waiting to tell the tale of how you stitched him up over a business deal, or there might be an angry ex-girlfriend out there somewhere."

"I've got nothing to hide."

"Everyone's got something to hide, Rob."

And she was right of course; we've all got some things we'd rather not see revealed in front of an audience of millions but I didn't see that as a valid reason for turning down a wonderful opportunity to help others, which is exactly what appearing on *Secret Millionaire* would be.

"Anyway, the producers may not want me for the programme once they've seen me; I might not be suitable."

"What do you mean, 'not suitable'?" H turned around and gave me a questioning look. "Why on earth wouldn't you be suitable?"

"I don't know, Jamie said they would have to see how I appeared on camera; whether I was comfortable being filmed, I suppose." I felt a distinct shift in H's attitude now that she thought it would be the production company turning me down rather than the other way round.

"You'd be fine on camera," she said firmly. "You speak well, you look good, and you've wanted to increase the time you spend on charity work for as long as I've known you. You'd be perfect." And I took that to be H's final word on the matter. She didn't really want me to do it, but she was blowed if someone else was going to give her husband the thumbs down.

I gave her a kiss on the cheek to show I understood and said I'd speak to Jamie in the morning. What I hadn't told H was that there was a distinct possibility that she would also have to be filmed for the show, assuming I was accepted of course, but I said nothing at this stage; I'd deal with that problem when I came to it.

A few days later Ditch drove me to London for a meeting with RDF Media where I was ushered into a large room. As

I sat down I was aware that there was a camera directed at me and for about 30 seconds I felt a little uncomfortable. But as soon as I started answering the questions fired at me, about my life, my family and any previous charity work I'd been involved in, I started to relax. I forgot about the camera and concentrated on giving a good account of myself instead, becoming quite animated in the process and I realised that I really wanted to do this; I wanted to appear on *Secret Millionaire.*

"What type of charity work or good causes would you like to get involved in?" was one of the first questions and I immediately told them about Horizon Children's Charity in Romania.

"I'd like to work with children," I said with certainty. "Anything that helps young people make their way in the world; whether it's through community work, sports or education, I don't mind."

I knew how much sport meant to me and my kids; I also knew how much we'd benefited from a good education. I wasn't sure I would have achieved as much in business without these two big influences in my life; that and having a loving family around me.

It all seemed to go well and a couple of hours later I was travelling back up north in the Bentley.

"What's *Secret Millionaire* all about then?" asked Ditch.

"It's a prime time, one hour programme; part entertainment, part social commentary," I replied, surprising myself at the accurate description.

"And how are you going to blend in with the people you're supposed to be helping?" asked Ditch looking in the rear view mirror at my reflection. I was wearing a hand-made pin-striped suit, pink shirt. My hair was expensively cut and I looked pretty fit and healthy, even though I say so myself.

"Well, if they give me the thumbs-up, I'm supposed to be an unemployed builder from Blacon looking for an opportunity to get into youth work."

Blacon is the least salubrious part of Chester with a higher crime rate than the rest of the city and a long way from the life H and I had created for ourselves at Fron Farm. "I'm supposed to be making a documentary about the process of setting up an establishment to help youngsters in the community. That's how we'll be explaining the presence of the cameras everywhere I go," I added.

Ditch looked doubtful.

"The production company could still turn me down," I added, glancing at my reflection and looking a bit doubtful myself. "But I hope they don't."

Next thing I knew, RDF was asking if someone from their offices could travel to Fron Farm to meet Helen.

"What do they want to meet me for?" she asked and I assured her it was only to talk about yours truly, so she agreed. I believe the questions she was asked were fairly in depth and H kept nothing back!

Pip, the director, Jeremy the cameraman and Oli the

sound technician came up to shadow me for a day, sitting next to me in the car and finding out exactly what I got up to all day as Ditch drove me from Fron Farm to Haycroft, from Haycroft to a meeting, from the meeting to Haycroft and from Haycroft back home again. It was invariably after 9.00pm by the time we pulled up outside Fron Farm.

"You're very busy, aren't you Rob?" asked Pip as the camera recorded my every move.

"Yes, but I'm used to it," I replied. "I'd feel guilty if I didn't work this hard. I've been given a lot of opportunities in my life; I feel that I have to make the most of them."

A week or so later, in September 2008, the call came telling me that I was just what the producers were looking for and would I like to appear on the programme. By now H was resigned to the fact I was going to be on TV and was prepared for it, but ironically I'm not sure I was. I knew I was being given an unprecedented opportunity to help people and I grabbed it with both hands, but I didn't give any thought to the effect the process of filming the programme would have on me as a person. In fact *Secret Millionaire* changed my life; just not necessarily in the way I imagined.

I was told we would be filming my episode just two months later in November and the only instructions I was given at this stage was to pack casual clothes for my trip.

"How long are you going for?" asked H.

"Nine days."

"And how much money will you have to live on?"

"Seventy seven pounds," I said, looking at the paltry amount of cash in my hand.

"That's impossible," said H, sounding totally incredulous and echoing my thoughts exactly.

"Seventy seven pounds is what a single adult person would receive in benefits for nine days if they were unemployed," I said by way of explanation. It was also the amount H and I could spend on a meal for two at our local pub.

I pulled on an old pair of jeans and a sweatshirt I'd bought that week in TK Maxx. According to the producers of the programme my usual casual outfits shouted 'country farmer' not 'inner city youth worker' so I'd had to buy a whole new wardrobe of hoodies and t-shirts.

H handed me my suitcase which the director had watched her pack. I assumed there was nothing in my case that could embarrass me, but I was just about to learn the first rule of television: Never assume anything.

"Where are we going?" I asked as I jumped into the car.

"We can't tell you, I'm afraid," came the reply, but I could see straight away that the SatNav was set for Liverpool so I sat back and watched the scenery go by, all the while trying to calculate how on earth I was going to survive for nine days on £77. I knew I had to pay all living expenses out of that, including my meals, which wasn't going to be easy to calculate since I wasn't even sure how much a pint of milk cost.

I was surprised when the car eventually pulled into John

The happy couple

Arriving in style at Skibo Castle on my 40th birthday

My pal Keith Mather, always there even through the tough times

Uncle Frank Banner, Graham Barclay and me

Left-right, Richard Buck of Pochin plc, Jan Ward, Shane Gibson, Chris Blowers/Investec, Anthony Pochin of Pochin plc and me

Taking time out!!!

Sir Leslie Young, Chairman of Eatonfield Group plc

Left-right, CEO Gatineau Andrew Bagley, Beverley Callard from Coronation Street with H and me at the open day at Eatonfield Day Spa

H at the Romania fund raising evening at the Grosvenor Hotel Chester

Left-right, Simona, three of the farm residents and H

Congratulations all round!

*At the Romania charity auction with H,
Jeff Winter, former FA Premier League
Referee and Jo*

Absailing in Wales for charity with H

At the Wellfield Shopping Centre with, left, Keith Williams, an RNLI representative and Brian, Shopping Centre Manager

With Terry Carroll on the announcement of the Eatonfield floatation

Eatonfield's ongoing relationship with the regeneration of Cardigan

My biggest deal to date, the Corus site in Workington

Bookham, Our quickest £5m profit deal

With Mum at Haycroft

Keith Mather, Paul King, Chris Caulfield and Simon Brown on a 'lads' night out in the Bahamas

*With trainer Lisa Williamson celebrating with Dream of Paradise after her
win at Chester*

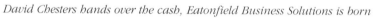

David Chesters hands over the cash, Eatonfield Business Solutions is born

Lennon Airport on the outskirts of Liverpool and I was told that I would be flying at 11am. I could see that there were two flights on the departure board for that time: Malaga and Belfast so I sat down and waited, convinced I was going to Belfast, a city everyone had heard of but no-one I knew had ever been to.

"Time to check in, Rob," said the director and I moved over to the desk, bringing my case with me.

"Too heavy I'm afraid," said the easyJet employee.

"Can you take something out?" asked Pip, so I unzipped the suitcase, not sure what H could have packed that had tipped it over the limit. As I rummaged through my jeans, t-shirts and recently bought sweatshirts I saw the glint of green glass and I knew immediately what my lovely wife had done. H had included a little treat to help me get through the hardship of nine days on £77; she'd packed a couple of bottles of Moet.

"You'll have to leave the champagne here, Rob," said Pip, camera running as she tried not to laugh and I handed over the offending items.

I was right; we weren't going to Malaga and once we'd landed at Belfast International Airport there was a taxi waiting for me, ready to take me to the Shankill Road area and my home for the next nine days.

"What do you know about Belfast, Rob?" I was asked and I had to say that I didn't know much. I'd grown up with stories of The Troubles constantly in the news but it hadn't affected my own life in the slightest. I knew that the

Catholics of Northern Ireland were represented by Sinn Fein and I remembered in the 70s that Gerry Adams' real voice was never broadcast. I also remembered the booming speeches of the fiery Ian Paisley, a favourite subject of impressionist Mike Yarwood. These were boyhood memories and now, 30 years later, here I was travelling through a city that seemed to me to be famous for one reason only; for the decades of violence and unrest.

We drove past Sinn Fein's headquarters as my taxi driver explained the continuing religious division in the city; Falls Road was on the catholic side and Shankill Road on the protestant side. The Peace Wall and other metal barricades ran right through the centre of the two neighbourhoods, separating one from the other. As I peered from the taxi window I felt a shiver go down my spine. I could just see the first row of houses on the protestant side of the wall; unoccupied from the day they were built because to live there would have been like living on the front line of a war zone. There were holes in the windows which could have been made by stones - or bullets, for all I knew - broken glass on the ground and vivid murals on the walls. There was one particular mural on a wall in the Shankill Road that caught my eye; a farmer on his tractor with his wife standing next to him, a typical image of the farming community and one that I could relate to, except in this instance the farmer's wife was holding a gun. It was a shocking sight, made even worse by the terrible poverty I could see everywhere I looked.

This was a city that in my view still looked as if it was at war.

As we drove closer to the terraced house that was to become my home for the next nine days, I knew first and foremost that the only way to improve matters in a place as badly damaged as Belfast was to get the two sides to communicate. I knew that any charity or project I was going to get involved in had to be a cross community one, one where Catholics and Protestants were encouraged to mix. I wanted to focus on my task, which was to help people, rather than have to get involved in the politics.

"This is it," said the taxi driver as the cab pulled up in front of a rundown terrace of houses, most of them boarded up. I grabbed my bag and jumped out on to the pavement, putting the key tentatively in the lock. Then as I crossed the threshold and stepped straight into the lounge my mind was immediately emptied of every single thing; from politics to charity work, from Falls Road to Shankill Road. All I could think of was how on earth I was going to live here for nine minutes, never mind nine days because it was pretty basic, to say the least.

CHAPTER TWENTY TWO

Secret Millionaire – take two

'I couldn't remember the last time a win at the races had been so important to me.'

The simple answer to the question of how on earth I was going to live in this two-up-two-down terraced house with its tiny kitchen and cramped living space was that I had no choice.

I unpacked my suitcase, two bottles of Moet lighter, then took a closer look. The carpet was stained, there was dust everywhere and, as far as I was concerned, the downstairs shower room needed ripping out and replacing. I can't stand dirt or mess of any description and this house was testing me to my limits. But I had to ignore it so I sat down on the battered sofa and spread my money out. I reasoned that if I kept breakfast to the absolute basics of toast and coffee and was very economical with the rest of my meals I might just survive.

The producers of the show knew the type of projects I wanted to get involved in and they had done a lot of research on my behalf, but I wanted to get a feel for the area myself and to do that I needed to meet the people who lived here. That evening, I nipped out to the local pub, The Royal, and ordered a pint of Guinness. Within the hour I was treated as if I'd been drinking there all my life.

"What brings you to the Shankill Road area of Belfast?" I was asked and I repeated the story that I'd agreed with the producers of the show; I was an unemployed builder hoping to switch careers and become a youth worker. I was looking for inspiring community projects with the intention of filming them and taking these good examples back with me to Chester.

I think I was pretty convincing. I didn't have any difficulty pretending to be a builder from a council estate, but I did have a problem with the small talk. I've never been very good at asking after people's families or discussing the weather and I struggled to hide that fact at times, something that Pip, the director, noticed too.

In fact, it was while I was trying my best to have a conversation with some of the other drinkers in the pub that the barman put another pint down in front of me.

"I didn't order this, did I?" I asked, looking up. I knew I couldn't afford another Guinness on my modest budget.

"No, but he did," said the barman, pointing to one of the locals I'd just been speaking to. Since it wasn't in my nature to accept a pint from someone and not return it, I had to down this one, then order another, which meant I had to leave The Royal pretty sharpish or I'd be completely spent up.

By the time I got back to the house at 9.30pm I'd blown £12 of my week's budget which was a bit of a disaster, to say the least.

The next morning I started my research on the charities and voluntary organisations that *Secret Millionaire* had found for me with the intention of visiting the ones that ticked all my boxes; I was interested in young people or children; the project had to have a broad appeal and most important of all, I wanted it to cross the boundaries with equal support for both the Catholic and Protestant communities.

The first charity I visited was a club run by a couple of impressive Irish characters; Tommy and Shoey. Shoey was as hard as nails and a man with a violent past but both he and Tommy now dedicated their lives to a cross community project aimed at keeping troubled young men off the streets. Situated on the Shankill Road, they were hoping to relocate to new premises smack bang in the middle of the Peace Wall but needed an injection of cash before they could move.

Shoey told me what had inspired him.

"I got caught up in some serious violence when I was younger," he explained, "And next thing I know, I'm down on the floor, badly injured, when I hear a voice speaking to me. I don't see anyone; I just hear the voice and it's telling me to go and help others in this city. When I get back on my feet again that's exactly what I decide to do."

Nothing could phase Shoey; violence, drugs, anti-social

behaviour - he'd seen it all before and both he and Tommy had a real empathy with everyone who came to the club. I really liked the set up and I liked the idea of investing in them. Pip, the director, seemed keen too, but I could only choose four of the projects on the list and I had a few more to see before I made my decision.

The Ardoyne area of Belfast is a Catholic enclave right in the middle of the Protestant part of the city, like a solid centre in a ring doughnut, and this is where I travelled the next day to meet Jackie.

Jackie runs the thriving John Paul's youth club for children aged five to 16. The club has facilities for indoor football, basketball, table tennis and pool. The building also has a tuck shop and an art room but as Jackie explained; they were now hoping to raise money to build a much needed dance studio as well. She showed me round the rest of the building and introduced me to a few of the youngsters as they threw themselves into everything that the club had to offer, both of us having to shout to make ourselves heard above the din.

"I'd also love to be able to provide a memorial garden for those quiet moments of reflection," said Jackie, which seemed a very attractive idea right now as the noise was deafening!

"I feel it would be a fitting tribute to my mum who started this club so many years ago," explained Jackie and I agreed with her; what a lovely legacy that would be. I was impressed by Jackie's enthusiasm and commitment to the kids but I was also touched by her desire to do something for her mum. Knowing how I felt about Sam, I could relate to Jackie's wishes completely.

From John Paul's youth club in the Catholic part of the city I saw Tom, an unemployed single dad who spent a lot of time at Cairn Lodge Boxing Club in the Protestant part of Belfast. Tom was Welsh but had been living in the city for many years with his 13-year-old son Nathan. He was also ill with emphysema and couldn't work, instead he dedicated his life to Nathan, stressing the importance of a good education and encouraging him to play an active part in the boxing club.

During the next few days I became quite close to Tom; his commitment to his son touched me deeply and I could tell that Nathan also thought the world of his dad. Tom owned very little, other than the clothes he stood up in, but nothing was too good for his son. It's difficult to buy the things a growing lad needs if you can't earn a decent wage, never mind buy a few luxuries. Once again, this was a situation that seemed to have parallels with my own life and I realised the researchers on the programme had really done their homework.

I was then introduced to Tommy who actually ran the boxing club with his son, Thomas. Apart from all sharing the same name, Tom, Tommy and Thomas all had this selfless desire to help others which for me, was incredibly humbling. Tommy volunteered at the club five days a week, 52 weeks of the year. The club was really important in the community; keeping the kids off the streets and teaching them discipline as well as showing them the importance of creating lasting friendships.

I discovered from Tommy that the club needed to raise a significant sum of money to help build new premises and my ears pricked up with interest. Once again Pip had done her research. Building property was something I had plenty of experience of and I knew I could offer advice as well as money.

Then there was 21-year-old Lucy, a qualified beauty therapist who'd occasionally lived rough in the Ardoyne area. Even though Lucy was ambitious she'd had a difficult life and had ended up in a Flax Housing Association hostel. Lucy also suffered from epilepsy and was having difficulty finding the right medication, but despite all this I could tell that she had the will to make something of her life, she just didn't have the means.

Through Lucy I met Marie who ran the hostel were Lucy lived; yet another hard working, completely unselfish individual who had dedicated her life to others. How on earth could I choose between them?

All six of the people and projects I'd visited were worthy recipients of my cash but I had to choose just four. I knew the director of *Secret Millionaire* was keen for me to pick the cross community youth project run by Tommy and Shoey and if you'd asked my opinion at the beginning of the week I would have agreed, but something Tommy had said to me about applying for a grant made me hesitate. I arranged for a return visit to see them both but before I could meet them again I realised that today was day four and I'd almost run out of money. There was no way the members of the production company were going to help me out so I had to think of a way to bolster my finances.

I did the only thing I could think of and called Chris O'Donnell my racing manager.

"Chris, I need a horse that's running today; any track, it doesn't matter."

Chris called me back ten minutes later and advised me to put a few quid on Icelandic which was running at Doncaster later that afternoon. I told the crew what I was doing and they were keen to film me walking into the betting shop. They knew it would make good TV – if the horse won.

I don't know who cheered loudest; me or them when Icelandic passed the winning post at odds of 11-1. I picked up my winnings, all £23 of it and breathed a huge sigh of relief, safe in the knowledge that I would just about make it to the end of the week. I couldn't remember the last time a win at the races had been so important to me.

I was being put under a bit more pressure now to make my choices but I was determined not to be rushed. Anyone who goes on *Secret Millionaire* has the power – literally - to change lives so it was important to me that I made the right decision. And it wasn't just who to choose, it was how much to give.

In the end, circumstances helped make the decision for me. Tommy and Shoey had indeed applied for a grant and I knew that any donation I made to their youth club could easily jeopardise their application. Even though initially I'd put a lot of emphasis on a cross community project, in the end it just wasn't meant to be.

I was about to travel to see Jackie at John Paul's youth club when I felt I had to explain to the crew that there was no way I was going to get emotional on camera. I told them that if I felt close to tears I knew I would have to leave the room. I was suddenly scared, not about telling the truth, but how I would feel when I did. It wasn't just about giving money away any more, it was about feeling something for the person I was giving the money to; it was caring for them and wanting the best for them. It had less and less to do with Rob Lloyd the millionaire, or Rob the youth worker but everything to do with the lives of these people I'd got to know in Belfast.

"When I reveal who I am, I don't want to say 'I'm a millionaire'," I announced.

The camera crew looked at me as if I'd gone mad. "But that's the whole point; the programme is called *Secret Millionaire*. If you don't actually say 'I'm a millionaire' it'll be meaningless."

"I don't want to say it. It sounds like I'm bragging." If I could have given everyone the money they deserved without the cameras in the room I think I would have been happier, which probably proves how emotional I was feeling at the time. As far as the programme makers were concerned I'd just thrown a big fat spanner in the works.

Calls were made to London while I kept tight hold of the cheques in my hand; an initial £20k for Tommy and Thomas' boxing club, with another £10k to follow, £10k for Jackie's youth club, £5k for Tom personally with a promise of £4k for Nathan's education in the future as well as £200 for every 'A' grade he achieved in his GCSEs and £5k for Lucy with a promise of a further £5k in a year's time if she could show she was capable of running her own business. In the meantime I'd be sending Steve Hopwood and his lads over to help with any building work required.

"You have to say 'I'm a millionaire'," said Pip, implying that there was no choice in the matter and I had to accept that she was probably right. I nodded and left the two-up-two-down terraced house for the last time, ready to tell Jackie, Lucy, Tom and Nathan, Tommy and Thomas that I wasn't a youth worker; I was in fact a millionaire.

CHAPTER TWENTY THREE

Time for reflection

'The process of making Secret Millionaire made me
realise that I'm actually a very selfish person, I'm a
workaholic and I can't – or won't – slow down.'

I was in Belfast for 10 days in total and the time away from home had taken its toll. It wasn't just the emotions that had been churned up after meeting all these deserving people, it was the fact that I'd been away from Eatonfield, Rob Lloyd Racing and most of all, H, for longer than I'd ever been before.

Before we'd even started filming the programme, I knew something in my life had to change because if it didn't my relationship with H would suffer irreparable damage. You can't have a relationship with someone you never see. We didn't have fun any more because I didn't have time to have fun. I'd come home from Haycroft Farm and I'd be too tired to eat. I'd go straight to bed, then get up at 5.30am and be back at the stables for 6am. I'd be checking all the horses, watching them go out on the gallops, talking to Pat, finding out if we'd had any enquiries from new owners or any staff problems in the yard. By 8.30am I'd be at my desk ready for a full day's work for Eatonfield. I'd work through till 7pm, 8pm, even 9pm and then travel back to Fron Farm to see H. I was exhausted and well on the way to complete burn out and I knew I had to make some serious changes.

All this was going through my mind as I was waiting to hand over the cheques. All of these people deserved my money but I had to narrow it down to four recipients.

In the end I decided not to contribute to the Flax Foyer, but I did go back there to see Lucy.

"I haven't been entirely honest with you, Lucy," I said, feeling a little nervous. "I'm not researching youth work in Belfast at all; I am in fact a successful property developer. I'm a millionaire." I watched as Lucy looked at me; confused and totally disbelieving and then I handed her the cheque. She looked down at it and then up at me in amazement.

"Five thousand pounds; you're kidding me right?" she said, and I had to keep assuring her that I wasn't. Lucy didn't know what on earth to say so I tried to explain that I thought that she'd be really good at running her own business as a beauty therapist. I told her that I liked her attitude and her positive outlook on life. "I know you'll make it work," I said.

The look on her face changed very gradually from one of total disbelief to one of gratitude until she eventually allowed herself a smile.

"Thank you. No-one's ever done anything like this for me before." And I don't think anyone had ever believed in her like this before either. I knew then that the last 10 days had been worth it.

Jackie at John Paul's youth club was also speechless but for a different reason. All she could think of was how much the youngsters were going to benefit from a dance studio.

"I've spoken to Steve Hopwood," I said, "And we'll have it completed for you by Christmas."

I then told her that I also wanted to help her construct the memorial garden for her mum and she was so touched I found my composure starting to crumble.

Keeping all these emotions at bay was beginning to get to me and it was Tom, Nathan's dad, who finally tipped me over the edge. With the camera crew in tow I travelled back to the Shankill Road to see them.

"Thanks for all your help this week, Tom," I said, as we stood in his lounge. "I've really enjoyed your company and I think you do a fantastic job bringing up your son on your own – however, I haven't been entirely honest with you."

According to the *Secret Millionaire* 'script' I was now expected to pause. As I looked at Tom I realised he had no idea what was going on.

"I'm not who I said I was; I'm not a builder and I'm not planning to start a boxing club in Cheshire. My name is Rob, but I'm not unemployed, I'm a millionaire."

Tom just stared at me as if I'd spoken in a foreign language, then once the emotions began to hit home his expression changed. As I gave the cheque to him the image of my dad was suddenly right there in front of me. Tom could have been Sam; both single parents, both bringing up their sons to believe that education and sport are ideal ways to help you succeed in life and both suffering from emphysema.

"I want you to have this to pay off your debts," I said and handed him the cheque for £5k.

Tom stepped forward to give me a hug and as he reached out to take the cheque the expression on his face cut me to the quick. Up until that moment I was coping – just – but the look on Tom's face was too much for me. I didn't want anyone to see me break down, least of all the camera crew and I had to leave the room.

Secret Millionaire wasn't about me any more; it was all about Tom and Nathan, Jackie, Lucy, Tommy and Thomas and I felt it was important for that reason to be in control of my emotions. It took me a while to compose myself and to feel able to carry on filming.

"And I want to give you £4k to help with Nathan's education in the future," I said, once I'd come back into the room. "With the added incentive of an extra £200 for each 'A' grade he achieves in his GCSEs."

Poor Nathan was completely speechless. It was all proving too much for him but I still had one more surprise up my sleeve.

"And just before I go, I'd like to give you these," I said. "Four VIP tickets for the Ricky Hatton Promotions' fight in

Bristol in December. I hope you won't mind if me and my son, Dan, come along with you."

Tom had always wanted to go to a professional boxing match and I took his and Nathan's smiles to mean that they wouldn't mind at all.

I then had to ask them both not to breathe a word to anyone. "I want to donate some money to the boxing club as well," I said. "So if you could keep it all quiet until we've been there this evening, I'd really appreciate it."

And they promised they would. We arranged to meet at the club at 6pm and I left Tom and Nathan stunned but hopefully, happy.

When we arrived at the club that evening it was full to capacity. I sat with Tommy and Thomas at the ring watching the sparring sessions while I waited for Pip to give me a nudge and instruct me to make my announcement.

I took my cue and began my explanation. "Tommy, I haven't been completely honest with you. I'm not here to research the process of starting up my own boxing club at all, I am, in fact, a successful property developer; I'm a millionaire." Once again, Tommy and Thomas just stared at me open-mouthed.

"And I've got a cheque for you both."

Poor Tommy could barely come to terms with it all. "Twenty thousand pounds," he said when I gave him the cheque, shaking his head in disbelief.

"With another £10k in a year's time," I explained.

There was a whole story in the look he gave me; it was full of gratitude, amazement and relief. He knew as well as I did that the club was going to go from strength to strength with that amount of cash. I don't think anyone had ever told Tommy what a wonderful job he was doing for the whole community but I hoped my gesture helped to describe what I thought of him personally. Having been with them now for over a week I was impressed, amazed and, if I'd lived in the Shankill Road and had a son who wanted to box, then I'd be extremely grateful too. Young Thomas kept putting his arm around me and shaking my hand. "I can't believe it," he said, over and over again.

Later that evening, Thomas handed me his green boxing gloves, the very ones he'd worn when he'd boxed for his country. "I've asked everyone to sign them," he said, as I looked at the signatures of all the people I'd met at the boxing club in the last 10 days and then it was my turn to be lost for words.

The process of making *Secret Millionaire* made me realise that I'm actually a very selfish person; I'm a workaholic and I can't – or won't – slow down. After a day working with Eatonfield I'll come home and H will say to me: "You're not in the boardroom now; this is me you're talking to, Rob." And she'll make me rethink my words and my tone of voice. I don't even know I'm doing it but it's obvious that the distinction between home and work was becoming blurred for me. That was just one of the things I knew I would have to change when I got back from Belfast.

The programme also made me think about changes that had already happened in my life, which I thought was an interesting side-effect of being away from home for 10 days.

When I first met H I had the upper hand; I was jealous and possessive and I don't think I was always as understanding or 'nice' as I could have been. I was in control of the relationship. Over the years, things have completely changed and H is very much in control now; I'm always on the back foot. I'd quite like to regain some of that higher ground but to do that I'd have to make more time for 'us' – and I will do, very soon.

What *Secret Millionaire* did was give me time to reflect. When I left Haycroft Farm for the trip to Belfast I didn't tell anyone that I was going away to film a TV programme. I said that if there was a problem with Eatonfield or with Rob Lloyd Racing I wanted it sorted out without me, I didn't want my daily 'phone call to the office to be anything other than an opportunity for everyone to tell me that things were fine and, believe it or not, that's exactly what happened. In the past, I've been convinced that if I'm not at the stables there will be a problem that only I can sort out or, if I'm not available at Eatonfield, something will go wrong with our latest deal which has proved to be a bit of a self-fulfilling prophecy. Perhaps Belfast proved to me that I could afford to take a break and that life does have the ability to go on quite successfully without me; I don't have to be constantly plugged in to my mobile 'phone to be the chief executive of a plc and I don't need to be a horse's reins away from

Haycroft at all times to run a successful racing stables. It was quite a revelation.

But before I say that I'm a completely reformed character, I have to come clean and say I've done nothing about these two revelations since. H would never forgive me if I lied about what I did next and the truth is I have done absolutely nothing; if anything I'm working more intensely than ever. The reason for this is that the current market is such a good opportunity to make money and I'm looking at potential deals on a daily basis, sometimes two or three a day. Looking forward, I can see the opportunity to take Eatonfield plc into a large company and I can't do that if I start to take a back seat.

Meanwhile Sir Leslie Young announced his intention to retire early the following year. He stated in our annual report that 2008 had been 'extremely difficult' for the property and construction sector. However, his optimism for the future prospects for Eatonfield were also made clear when he said that we were hopeful of a significant profit from two sites, Paignton (the Bookham deal) and Corus, which we hoped would be realised in the financial year to June 30, 2010 once we'd secured planning.

In November 2008 Howard Jones resigned to take up a new post with a company in Scotland and in January 2009 I had to make a further loan of £400k to meet Eatonfield's short-term cash problems. The loan was to be unsecured and free of interest and repayable on demand or by February 26th. The other two directors, Suki Kalirai and Sir

Leslie consulted with Evolution Securities and it was considered that the terms of the transaction were fair and reasonable insofar as the company's shareholders were concerned. I was the only one in a position to forward the cash as the current trading conditions meant that it was almost impossible to obtain finance from the banks. I was also very aware that I'd only been able to launch Rob Lloyd Racing thanks to the success of Eatonfield, so it seemed fitting that Rob Lloyd Racing should be there in Eatonfield's time of need.

The loan doesn't worry me because I know that hopefully in the next few years Eatonfield will be making serious money again and I also know that 90% of property businesses out there are struggling at the moment due to the write down on their property assets. All they can do is hope that the banks will stand by them until the market improves. Every time I look at a property or development site now I think exactly as a bank would think and that's why buying at the right price is very, very important. I'm finding that if I put in a low offer, sellers don't always dismiss it out of hand.

When buying in this market there are a couple of points to bear in mind. Firstly, you shouldn't pay too much attention to valuations. Banks have to have valuations, I know, but I believe that's why the system has gone belly-up in the first place; valuations have been too high. I'm always cautious; I look at a site and say: 'What is it worth to me?' Forget the valuation and keep beating the price down.

If I look at 10 sites a day, I'll only make two or three offers, which could be derisory and will probably be declined – at first.

Secondly, just because the price has come down doesn't mean it's a good deal; you have to find your exit route. It's exactly the same as with bloodstock; top quality will always find a buyer. Good property with good tenants will always find a buyer but you still have to have a plan if the market goes pear-shaped. If you'd been offered the chance of an income producing development at the beginning of 2007, for example, with Lehman Bros as tenants, you would probably have been planning a relaxed retirement sooner rather than later, confident that your investment was a good one. But then on September 15th 2008 Lehman's filed for chapter 11 bankruptcy, the largest bankruptcy filing in US history. Nothing's safe any more.

I predict that *The Sunday Times Rich List* (published in April every year) will have more than a few omissions from the worlds of property and finance but I also predict that these companies and individuals will bounce back – as long as they have kept the banks informed. The secret is knowing when the market will start to pick up and when to begin investing again. Eatonfield has kept the banks informed at all times; we have also sold some stock to free up cash and I know the banks are ready to invest with us when the time is right. I think that will be some time around the middle of 2009 and when we do take the leap I want to invest in the bigger £50m to £100m deals subject to obtaining the right capital investment. I've learnt over the years that it's easier to go large and then you only need the market to alter slightly in the next year or two to make a profit. Banks know that this is a market I'm good at. And with that in mind the next three to five years will be crucial, not just for Eatonfield but for Rob Lloyd Racing too.

CHAPTER TWENTY FOUR

Horses for courses and a horse for Helen

'It was as if someone was looking down on us and saying: 'You've had such a tough time of it; we're going to give you a chance now'.'

At the beginning of 2009 trainer Pat Morris, or the Horse Whisperer as I call him, joined Rob Lloyd Racing from the Curragh, bringing with him a number of Irish owners. At the same time, bloodstock agent Bobby O'Ryan continued to look for horses for us, buying those that suited our budget and our requirements which meant we were now full to capacity in the main barn. It was time to think about expanding.

Fortunately, we had just enough room for the five horses arriving that week, one of which was Dreamcatcher; the horse that Bobby had found for H. All I had to do was wait for the perfect moment to tell her. Since I'd promised my wife that I would teach her to ride this would mean that we would be spending time together and that could only be a good thing. H had the boots, the hat and the jodhpurs;

Dreamcatcher was the final and most important part of the equation. He was 19 years old, an ex-racehorse, solid, dependable and the double of Desert Orchid. He was also more than 17hh, which I didn't see as a particular problem.

"But you've been around horses for 40 years, Rob; of course it's not going to worry you. I've never been on a horse in my life," said H, when I told her the news. She said he was far too big; I told her he would teach her all she needed to know. She promised she would try.

"You'll be teaching me to ride, won't you?" she asked. "I don't want anyone else in the yard to see how nervous I am."

"Of course," I replied.

"Because I'm warning you, the minute you hand me over to someone else because you're 'too busy' or you need 'five minutes to take a call' I'll be whipping off those jodhpurs, faster than you ever thought possible." She paused for a moment. "What are you smiling at?"

"Just thinking about you whipping off your jodhpurs," I said and we both laughed. For the first time in ages I realised we were actually having fun.

Appearing on *Secret Millionaire* had been an overwhelming experience and it took me a while to get back to normal. The weight of responsibility I felt when choosing who to give money to was difficult to come to terms with because it was up to me to decide who I felt was the most deserving. Everyone I met on the programme could have fulfilled that criterion.

As promised, I asked Steve Hopwood if he would go to Belfast to help Jackie build the dance studio and the memorial garden. Steve didn't have to go; it wasn't part of his job description, but he's a loyal employee who has been with me for more than 20 years and he didn't hesitate. Steve travelled to Belfast with Moi, our landscape gardener and Eddie the joiner, meeting up with a group of local builders and they all got stuck in, completing a 10 day job in four days. My £10k gift had probably cost me twice that amount, but it didn't matter; John Paul's youth club finally had what it needed.

I made a return visit to Belfast with RDF Media just before Christmas. Since my first visit to the city I'd had time to think about Lucy's future and I'd decided that she would benefit from a training period with a local hairdresser. I told her she should still use the money I'd given her to set up her own business but she needed to build up a client base first. I contacted Andrew Mulvenna a top class hairdressers in the centre of Belfast and he agreed to take Lucy on, with me funding her training for three months.

When I gave Lucy the news she was absolutely thrilled, in fact I think she was even more impressed with the three months in the salon than she was with the £5k cheque!

Tom and Nathan's trip over here to watch the Ricky Hatton promotion fights also went down well. Dan and I travelled to Bristol to meet them and the four of us had a great time, all dressed to the nines in black tie and dinner jackets. Ditch picked Tom and Nathan up at their hotel and drove them to the venue, which they told me was a great start to the night since neither of them had ridden in a Bentley before.

By the time Ricky Hatton came over to our table to meet us all, 13-year-old Nathan was so overcome we were having difficulty getting a word out of him.

There was a charity auction after the fight and I decided it would be a really good idea to have a permanent reminder of the whole experience. When I saw the Joe Calzaghe signed shorts and framed photo set I knew it would make an ideal gift for Tom and Nathan; like Calzaghe, Tom is originally from Wales.

I started the bidding at £120. Before long it was up to £400, then £420, with me finally clinching it at £500. We all watched as the two glamorous girls came towards our table, carrying the huge frame.

"Oh, it's not for me," I said. "It's for that young lad there." And I pointed to Nathan who could only stare at me, speechless. He and Tom then posed for a few extra photos with the framed shorts and Ricky Hatton. It was a brilliant end to a fantastic night.

The purpose of *Secret Millionaire* is to help people and I hope I've done that to some extent, but the side effect I hadn't bargained for was the time I spent thinking about my own life. I realised I had to do something if I was going to spend more time with H and I came up with a five year plan. I was going to work flat out for the next five years and then I was going to slow down a little. By then, J, Jo and Dan might want to get involved in the business themselves and allow me more time with my wife.

Speaking of which, H's second riding lesson at Haycroft Farm didn't go well.

"But Dreamcatcher doesn't want to turn left," said H crossly as she gripped hold of the reins. I tried to tell her that she had to be firm and show him who was boss.

"I've tried that before, and it doesn't work," she said, glaring at me. I knew what she was referring to and it wasn't the horse. H had told me on more than one occasion that she wanted me to work fewer hours and spend more time at home doing the things that normal couples do; having dinner together, seeing friends, starting a conversation and finishing it. "It's as if you've got another woman," she said sadly.

I wanted to do all those things too but, on the other hand, I felt as if I had no choice; I needed to work these 16 hour days. There were so many people relying on me now and I couldn't afford to let them down. The other problem was; I assumed everyone was as obsessed as I was, I forget that people don't have a one-track mind like me. I thrive on pressure but while my ambition was showing no signs of receding it simply wasn't true that I was happy with the situation; I wasn't, in fact H and I were both thoroughly miserable.

And then Rob Lloyd Racing suddenly stepped up a gear and any good intentions I had of changing my hectic lifestyle had to be put on the back burner yet again.

It was a beautiful morning in late January. The sun was

shining and the frost was hard on the ground. Chris O'Donnell and I were standing with some of the owners who had come to Haycroft for one of our regular Saturday morning breakfasts. Mac was there to watch his three-year-old filly, Moneysupermarket, as was David Pickering, one of the directors of Chester Racecourse and a non-executive director of Meadow Foods Ltd. He was there with friends to see Admiral of the Dee and Miss Dee Lady, two of the horses in their four horse syndicate. David has been a wonderful support to me since the beginning, sticking with us when times were bleak. Even in the dark days when we were sending horses to other trainers David didn't waver and I will always be grateful to him for that.

So, I was really enjoying myself; in fact we were all getting a buzz out of seeing the horses making their way towards us. I enjoy everything about racing and leaning against the white railings of the gallops on a Saturday morning always reminds me why I'm addicted to what is both a ridiculously expensive pastime and a relentless pursuit for perfection.

We watched them coming out of the yard, a string of beautiful thoroughbreds, nostrils flaring, all on their toes, as they made their way to the open countryside. Then within sight of Peckforton Castle and Beeston Castle they took off into the distance, jostling for position, straining on the bit to go faster.

Afterwards, we all stood having breakfast together in the owners lounge; a few glasses of fizz and a bacon bap.

Racing is a sociable sport and it's important to enjoy being an owner, but ultimately, we're here to win. Rob Lloyd Racing isn't a yard that pins its hopes on having a runner at Wolverhampton or Musselburgh every now and again; we're aiming for the best tracks and we have quite a few horses in training that are on target for big things.

The 'phone was ringing every day now with new enquiries from potential owners, which was fantastic given that we were officially in a recession. I'd heard that other trainers were making cutbacks but we were doing the opposite. It was as if someone was looking down on us and saying: 'You've had such a tough time of it; we're going to give you a chance' and it was great; I was so committed and so passionate it seemed that I was getting my reward.

I was discussing all this with Mac when my mobile rang. It was Pat and he was in Ireland. He wanted to talk to me about the Sheikh.

Sheikh Haif Mohammed Al-Qhatani's horses had been with Pat Morris for a number of years at the Curragh. When Pat moved to join Rob Lloyd Racing in January he brought one of the Sheikh's horses with him, Absher, a colt by Noverre. We knew the Sheikh had a massive bloodstock business as Bobby had bought a very promising colt by Bahamian Bounty from him in the past.

"The Sheikh's agent is very happy with Absher's progress so he's decided to send two more horses over to Haycroft," said Pat.

I took on board the importance of what Pat was telling

me. This was a real coup, to say the least. It was like receiving a cheque on *Secret Millionaire* instead of giving one. As an owner of a racing stables this was a dream come true.

At the last count I had now spent another £500k on top of the original £4m investment at Haycroft but, at long last, that investment was starting to reap dividends and as everyone in this business knows: All it takes is one horse...

One horse that proved to be a fabulous return on his owner's investment was Cockney Rebel. I told the story of this marvellous wonder horse to Michael Green, owner of Green Spirit and I think it's worth repeating here.

Cockney Rebel cost £30k as a yearling and was trained at Geoff Huffer's yard in Newmarket. In May 2007 he won the 2,000 Guineas as a 25-1 chance, followed three weeks later, by another stunning win in the Irish 2,000 Guineas at the Curragh. Phil Cunningham, owner of the Cockney Rebel syndicate, was said to have had an offer of £10m straight after the Irish which would have been a phenomenal return on his initial investment if he'd decided to take it up. Instead he chose to enter the horse in the St James Palace Stakes at Ascot in September where Cockney Rebel sustained a pelvic injury. Huffer was just getting the horse back on its feet when he suffered a freak accident on the gallops and the decision was taken to retire him to stud. In his short career the horse won almost £450k in prize money.

"Wonderful story, Rob. Do you have a horse here with

that sort of promise?" asked Michael.

"Not yet," I said with a smile. "But Phil Cunningham used bloodstock agent, Bobby O'Ryan, who just happens to buy all our horses for Rob Lloyd Racing."

And before Michael could digest that information, my 'phone bleeped with the arrival of a text message. I looked down; it was from H.

"So lonely without you. Don't be late tonight. All I want is to be with you, love H xxxxxx."

And I texted back: *"Me too. R xxxxx."*

CHAPTER TWENTY FIVE

The future for Eatonfield

'You have to play the numbers game. Don't come to me with 20 deals; come to me with 200 deals.'

I might have to accept that I'm not always the best husband in the world but, according to business colleagues, I am the best 'peerer over hedges' they've ever come across. Friends in the industry understand that I can often find a deal where others haven't even looked and by February 2009 equity providers were interested in investing with Eatonfield again; not only did they see that I'd shown commitment and belief in the company with my personal injections of cash in the last six months, they also knew that Eatonfield's greatest strengths lay in acquiring land at the best price, as well as obtaining planning on a development where other people had failed, thanks to the skills and tenacity of Planning Director, Steve Jones.

But the one development where I felt we hadn't succeeded was in Cardigan and it irritated me.

"Our day will come," I said to Steve, and neither of us

doubted it, the difficult bit was how long we might have to wait.

In November 2005 Eatonfield had sold most of its interest in Cardigan to Modus Properties for £6.275m. In 2003 I felt that Cardigan was an excellent investment and in my opinion it still was, I also firmly believed that Eatonfield was one of the few property companies that would succeed in getting planning permission. The town was still undeveloped, the chief executive of the council had changed but the town had not moved on. The ball needed picking up and I wanted Eatonfield to be the developer to run with it, so in 2008 we exchanged contracts to buy half of it back because I knew that it had enormous potential.

In five years time I will be 50 years old. In five years time I want to spend more time with my family and with Rob Lloyd Racing, which means I have five years to build Eatonfield up into the transformational company I've always dreamed of. And I know it can be done in today's market because there is so much distressed stock out there and also, crucially, because we still have the support of our banks.

There was a tower block in Manchester recently; 168 residential units, reduced in price from £34m to £15m. I put in an offer of £10m, a figure that I know I can raise. The banks aren't stupid; they're backing Eatonfield because they know I've put money in to the company myself and, as I've said, it's a good time to buy.

Unfortunately, a Dubai investor stepped in with an offer

of £15m, but let's wait and see; if the deal doesn't go through I'll be back.

Make no mistake, I fully appreciate the severity of the downturn in the property market but, from a personal point of view, I have every reason to feel confident. I have almost 50% share in Eatonfield as well as 50% profit share in Corus and Birkwood. Twelve months is a long time and the outlook could be very different in a year. I'm the first to admit that there have been quite a few changes with my own approach to the property business in the last 12 months: I thought that having satellite offices and more staff would take the pressure off me personally; I thought there would be less emphasis on me doing the deals and I would be able to rely on my land managers to find the right investments, but that didn't happen. I still had to do the deals myself because I discovered I was better at it than anyone else. So Eatonfield is going back to its roots; to a smaller, more focused company, concentrating on fewer but bigger deals. I will be treating staff more like fee earners than employees in the future and I'm going to get involved in every deal we do. As I've explained to J, you have to know a deal inside out; you have to live and breathe it and not everyone is prepared to do that. From buying my first properties in Pwllheli and Colwyn Bay, to the 87 acre, £180m re-development Corus site in Workington you need to know everything there is to know about the development and you have to be sure that if you buy it today, you can sell it tomorrow at a profit. I know I could have sold Corus a week after Eatonfield bought it for twice the amount we paid, but it's not enough, because I know that Corus will be a massive deal, one of the best we've ever done.

We also have £1.5m in escrow in the Paignton development. In order to get our money out I would have to buy the £10m bank debt, but as there is an offer on the table at the moment from Asda for £27.5m for a small part of the development, this could be considered a good deal. It's all about hanging on in there at the moment. I'm sure our day will come.

In mid-February I held a meeting with Keith Mather, Phil Middlehurst and Eatonfield's new FD, Paul Williams to discuss the future plans for the company. The outcome of our discussion was obvious: Due to the current economic climate we would have to reduce our overheads even further with survival being the key word.

We no longer had the cost of Eatonfield's head office in North Wales and we'd already made redundancies when moving staff to Haycroft but it was clear that we had to cut costs even further. It's never easy telling people that their services are no longer required, but we had no choice; we had to become leaner to survive.

Fewer staff meant there was more responsibility for Eatonfield's remaining employees, but for me that's not a problem. I've been told on many occasions that I'm one of the best dealmakers there is and it's important that I live up to investors' expectations. The thing is; I don't find it difficult; I can see the deals more easily than most, but even so it doesn't mean that Eatonfield hasn't struggled. Our interim results to December 2008 showed a loss of £7m with our share price at the end of February standing at 4p. But we have survived where so many others haven't for the simple reason that I have been determined not to let the banks down; I didn't in 1994 and I haven't now, 15 years later.

Banks are like elephants; they never forget. If I was to walk into the bank tomorrow and say: "I can't keep up the loan repayments, here's the keys to the company, make me bankrupt" and then walk away again it would be doing Eatonfield a terrible disservice and it would be very difficult in the future to regain the bank's confidence. What I'm saying to the banks instead is: "This is a good market for me, lend me another £30m, £40m, £50m and let's go." Don't forget, banks have to make money and it's easy to do the sums; with intro fees, exit fees and interest payments banks can and do make 30% on a deal if they put in capital as well as debt.

I was offered a development recently for £28m. Just six months ago it had been valued at £54m but it wasn't cheap enough as far as I was concerned. I know I can make £10m profit on a bad day, so I won't pay more than £22m. As I say, you have to ignore valuations.

The next deal is very important for Eatonfield and there are people I speak to in the property business on a regular basis who will help me make sure that the deal is the right one. People like Simon Brown.

Simon used to work at Evolution Securities, the brokers who took us through the AIM float. Simon is now with Matrix and I try to speak to him every day. He will occasionally put me in touch with other lenders.

"Have you spoken to Nick Leslau?" asked Simon recently, referring to the Chairman and Chief Executive of the Prestbury Group. I came across Nick for the first time when I was working for Grimley & Son in 1983 and he was MD of the Burford Group. Nick had negotiated to buy Piccadilly Plaza from Eagle Star and I was helping to attract tenants. I never forgot the fact that just five years later Nick sold the Plaza for £20m, immediately becoming an inspiration for me in the property business. In 2008 Nick appeared in the third series of *Secret Millionaire*.

"I haven't seen Nick for about nine months," I told Simon, remembering a brief meeting I had with him in London.

"Well, Nick's got cash – lots of cash," said Simon.

I thought back to when we'd met, when Nick said that he might be interested in doing a deal with Eatonfield. Of course, the Prestbury Group is a much bigger company than we are but I have every intention of approaching Nick again, once the timing is right.

In the meantime we have been approached by banks asking if Eatonfield Homes, the residential arm of the company, is interested in building out repossessed sites and sorting out planning problems. It's something for us to consider and demonstrates, I believe, that Eatonfield is now well known for its ability to trade on its strengths. Eatonfield is a successful brand.

We've also had equity funds approach us. One company expressed an interest in putting in £10m if we found a deal with £20m of debt; in effect a £30m vulture fund. Again it's something to consider.

On a personal level, I've been asked if I would be interested in running a city fund but this is one business deal that is definitely not an option for me; it would mean leaving the Northwest to live in London and I'm too committed to Eatonfield and my family to even consider it, but it's flattering nevertheless.

I suppose the big question is: why has Eatonfield survived when so many other property developers have not? Well, for a start I've always kept something back. For instance, after we'd floated the company we put £500k in a separate account as an emergency fund. We've always had something we could sell or raise money on quickly, such as a piece of land with no debt attached. My other piece of advice to those in the property business would be, don't mortgage yourself to the hilt; something I learnt after the failure of LPI.

I believe the advice I've been giving to J over the last 12 months is the best advice I could give to anyone. Jason is doing what I was doing 25 years ago; he's scouring the receivership market for distressed sales and building up a database with information from the banks. I've told him: "You have to play the numbers game, J. Don't come to me with 20 deals; come to me with 200 deals."

To find the right deal you have to keep checking on your

database; go through every single development to see if the price is coming down or if it has sold. Have 300 to 500 properties in that database at any one time and monitor them closely. Eventually you will find there is one deal you can 'nick'.

Remember; it's not rocket science, but bear in mind too that the next deal is the most important. I've repeated this advice to J over and over again and I've also told him that:

a) He needs a couple of banks behind him. When I was running the LPI Group I had just one; Lloyds Bank and

b) He needs to diversify. I wanted to be an empire builder in the early days with a massive portfolio but I'm now telling J it's safer to 'nick' that perfect deal, sell it and bank the profit. Build your business sensibly.

Don't forget, I was starting from ground level, whereas J's got me to advise him and I won't let him make a mistake. In fact, I'll probably be keeping an eye on him for the next 10 years, which is ironic, because Sam never gave me one word of advice in his whole life.

What Sam taught me instead was the importance of hard graft and that I should never give up. In fact without those two basic philosophies I doubt Rob Lloyd Racing would have got off the ground in the first place, never mind become a successful training establishment. Even with Sam gone, he continues to be an influence on me.

CHAPTER TWENTY SIX

The future of Rob Lloyd Racing

'Making a success of your life is not just about working hard; sometimes you need help in overcoming a problem because real life can get in the way of ambition.'

I love the calmness of the stables early on a Saturday morning as the sun comes up over the gallops. Peckforton Castle and Beeston Castle rise out of the mist, reminding me why I set up Rob Lloyd Racing in the village of Spurstow in the first place. There's nothing to beat it. I'll talk to Pat as he gives me the run down on which of the horses is on good form and I'll spend time meeting the owners as we wait for their horses to come out onto the gallops. I don't think I'll ever lose that sense of awe as I watch them thunder past, the ultimate in power and speed.

There's no doubt that Rob Lloyd Racing is a labour of love but what I have to keep reminding myself is that it's also a business.

Running a racing stables is a notoriously difficult business in which to make money but I have a bloody-minded attitude to those who say it can't be done. From a standing start and after just 18 months hard graft, Rob Lloyd Racing is a force to be reckoned with. We've got a five star establishment with the best of everything and a full yard of 60 horses and counting; we've got a sheikh owner, the first in Cheshire and we've got a top class trainer in Pat Morris. I've put in plans with the council to expand the stables and even had a discussion regarding the heli-pad with an acknowledgment that a couple of flights a year might be acceptable. I'm hoping for more of course, but at least it's a start.

I continue to be emotionally attached to a lot of the horses at Haycroft but that's because I have a personal interest in quite a few of them, none more so than Winrob. Named for me and Sam and it has run twice, Bobby bought this now three-year-old gelding at the breeze-up sales in Doncaster for £58k. Nothing would give me more pleasure than seeing Winrob win a race.

I also have Mary and Teddy West, two horses that race in my mother's colours; red with a white disc and red and white half sleeves. She was on the 'phone only last week saying she would love either of them to win a race, any race. "It'd be great to see them first past the post," she said and I know the feeling exactly. As we come up to our first full season on the flat I can feel the anticipation mounting.

We've also got Schoolboy Champ, jointly owned by Rob Lloyd Racing and J's Waterstown Club. The horse is very good looking – and he knows it! In fact we took the decision to geld him last month since he was finding it difficult to concentrate on the task in hand.

And then there's Lisa Appleton and Mario Marconi's syndicate horse, Bebenine, proof that horse racing appeals to all sorts of people that you wouldn't usually associate with the sport. Lisa and Mario got together on *Big Brother* in front of millions of viewers and have since been bitten by the racing bug. As I've said before; racing is about enjoying yourself but it's also about winning and I know that Rob Lloyd Racing has got to deliver; it's the only way to attract owners.

J has been helping to raise our profile with a number of marketing projects one of which was a particularly successful 'name the horse' competition on the local radio station, Dee 106FM. The presenter was inundated with suggestions over a period of five days and in the end we chose the name Lord Carling Boy, which is actually an anagram of Rob Lloyd Racing – very clever.

We've also had visits from local celebrities such as Nick Hancock and Kerry Katona which has kept our name in the papers and we've had an independent production company making a film of the story of Haycroft Farm; from the early days when Rob Lloyd Racing was just a collection of run down farm buildings to the five star establishment we've become today.

Anyone who has read my story so far will realise that I don't do things by halves and that I thrive on pressure. If I come up against a problem I don't tend to worry about it, I do something about it, but appearing on *Secret Millionaire* meant I slowed down for once in my life and I had time to be a bit more introspective. I saw the deprivation in Belfast; I saw evidence of the decades of violence and the friction between communities but I also saw the hard work that people like Jackie and Tom were doing and I saw hope for the future in Lucy and Nathan. Meeting them all made me realise that making a success of your life is not just about working hard; sometimes you need help in overcoming a problem because real life can get in the way of ambition. After *Secret Millionaire* I began to apply that principle to my own life; it was time to accept that I couldn't solve all my problems on my own.

I know that Rob Lloyd Racing will always have a special place in my heart but I know in my head that I have to concentrate on Eatonfield for the foreseeable future because without Eatonfield there would be no Rob Lloyd Racing. I'm always available at Haycroft on Saturdays because the owners expect to see me, but I know it's time now to let Pat Morris take over most of the responsibility for the racing yard with J.

Pat is 32 years old and joined us in January after a successful 10 years as a trainer at the Curragh. He's settled in well at Haycroft, not only is he quietly impressed with the level of investment in the stables, but his fiancée Sharon Pettigrew is originally from Cheshire and if there's one thing I've learned in the last few years it's that if the woman you love is happy, the rest of your life has more chance of falling into place.

Pat brought a few of his own horses with him from Ireland and they are quite a contrast to some that we'd bought for Rob Lloyd Racing. One of our three-year-olds, Best Bidder, cost €150k as a two-year-old and here was Pat showing me a six-year-old gelding that cost a whole lot less.

"This is Radiator Rooney," he said, stroking the nose of a calm bay. "He's won three races in the last 12 months and he cost me £1k as a three-year-old."

I looked at the massive head of Radiator Rooney as he nuzzled my hand. "He's also the friendliest horse in the world," said Pat. I stared up at his milky brown and white eye, the result of an injury when he was a foal and I was impressed. It just goes to show that you don't necessarily have to spend a lot of money to have a winner.

Then to prove that Radiator Rooney wasn't a fluke, Pat took me round the other side of the barn were the fillies were stabled and introduced me to Ask Jenny, who also cost £1k and had netted Pat a total of £20k in prize money in the last three years.

"If you're an owner you get a buzz out of winning no matter which track you're on," said Pat and I knew what he meant. Neither Radiator Rooney nor Ask Jenny was going to be running at Ascot or Newmarket at any stage in their career. Nevertheless, Pat knew that my ambitions for Rob Lloyd Racing included all the top class tracks. It also included the one ambition that had eluded me so far; a runner at Aintree and he'd promised to keep a look out for that one special horse with enough promise and potential to tackle the greatest National Hunt race of all time: The Grand National.

Whether it's horses for the National Hunt or horses for the flat, success breeds success. Everyone wants to win and key to that is communication; communication between the trainer, the head person and the owners, which is why I love to come down to Haycroft on Saturday mornings to find out for myself what's going on. I have no problem sweeping the snow off the gallops in the depths of winter and I have no problem disciplining one of the lads in the yard if that's what's required. The truth is; I don't like asking others to do what I wouldn't do myself and as H says: that's my big problem. It's no wonder really that quality time at home has become so rare because I find it very difficult to put a halt on my ambition; once I've started something I want to do it to the best of my ability and running a stables involves a lot more than just giving Bobby O'Ryan an unlimited pot of money to buy bloodstock. As Pat proved with his two thousand pound winners; it's not just about the money.

Speaking of which, the prize money in racing in the UK is notoriously low. If I was dependent on the prize money for the future of Rob Lloyd Racing we'd go bankrupt. The value comes out of the bloodstock and that's why Bobby O'Ryan is an important part of the process. If only Rob Lloyd Racing could discover a colt with the promise of Cockney Rebel I'd feel we'd finally arrived. Now that really would be raising the bar!

But while we wait for that horse of a lifetime we're making the most of the horses we already have at Haycroft Farm, getting them race fit and looking forward to this year's turf season. We're getting more and more enquiries as time goes on and I don't want to turn owners away so we've submitted plans to the council for more stables to accommodate an extra 34 horses. We've also put in plans for a new owners' block overlooking the gallops which will be a two storey glass and brick building with bar facilities. We have a waiting list developing for owners now, partly because of the network of contacts I've built up over the years and partly because Pat Morris is attracting interest from Ireland.

We're moving in the right direction but, if I'm honest, it's still tough going and like most businesses in these difficult economic times, racing has got its problems. I've had to dip into my cash reserves as I still own a number of horses myself and I have to pay training fees like every other owner but I'd rather do that than sell our bloodstock at a loss. We've done everything we can to ensure survival – a classic winner aside - and we're now expanding cautiously.

With Eatonfield and Rob Lloyd Racing now on the same premises I can make the most of my time without having to commute between Haycroft in Cheshire and Eatonfield in North Wales. We moved out of Eatonfield's head office in Mold in 2008 and I can now walk between one business and the other in a matter of minutes. I'm busier than ever, but I'm using my time more productively and it's also meant I can spend time with J and Jo as they enjoy working at Haycroft almost as much as me.

In the future I've no doubt that H will continue to persuade me to cut back on my workload and I know in my heart of hearts that I have to listen to her. She wants to spend more time with me and I want to spend more time with her, it's as simple as that. But achieving it at the moment is another matter. Eatonfield is about to enter a new phase in its development with the property market awash with opportunities for distressed sales. We might not get another chance like this for years; a market that allows us to increase the size of our deals tenfold. Meanwhile, Rob Lloyd Racing continues to fill me with passion and ambition.

CHAPTER TWENTY SEVEN

My future

'I think the secret of my life, if there is one, has been in believing in my goals and taking chances and opportunities when they've been presented to me.'

In mid-March I came back from a flying visit to Belfast having had a very productive meeting with the city council. If a suggested partnering scheme with the council gets the go-ahead then other communities will be able to use the proposed new centre for Cairn Lodge Boxing Club which, in turn, means that there is more chance of an application for lottery money gaining approval. All Tommy and Thomas need to do is ensure Cairn Lodge is in control of the land ownership and that planning permission on the scheme is obtained.

While I was in Belfast I also suggested canvassing local businesses and trade suppliers for materials in preparation for the start of the building work and I made it known that I wanted to get personally involved in that side of things too. In fact, the more I get involved in what's going on with the projects in Belfast, the more I enjoy it. The people are great and I don't just mean the individuals I've met on *Secret Millionaire;* I've been welcomed in the city wherever I go.

On my last visit Tom informed me that there was a waiting list of at least 50 youngsters who all wanted to join Cairn Lodge. "But we don't have the room, Rob," he told me.

Well, hopefully they soon will have, because I'm determined to get that club built for them. Nathan is still a committed member but unfortunately the day I was there I wasn't able to ask him how he was getting on.

"He wanted to have a day off school to come and see you," explained his dad, "But I couldn't let him do that now, could I?"

Well, no, I understand that his education is much more important – because that's exactly what Sam would have said to me.

I also managed to catch up with Lucy who had already spent three weeks training at Andrew Mulvenna. She'd obviously settled in well because she looked happy and confident and appeared to be making the most of the opportunity she'd been given.

"She's very professional," said Andrew. "She just needs to focus on building up the number of clients and she'll do well."

If Lucy listens to Andrew and realises he's on her side, I've no doubt she'll make a success of it and eventually realise her ambition of starting her own business. I've told her not to rush; she needs to make sure the time is right and when that time comes I've promised another £5k to help out.

All in all, *Secret Millionaire* has been a totally rewarding experience, but one that I didn't realise would be so intense. I'll be keeping in touch with everyone I've met in Belfast because I want to, not because I have to and I'll be hoping that Lucy, Jackie, Tom, Nathan, Tommy and Thomas will all keep in touch with me. They've all been given an opportunity; it's up to them now to make the most of it and I'm confident they all will.

As for opportunities in the property industry; they are still quite hard to come by simply because of the lack of available cash. Anyone who has got money is holding on to it, anyone who hasn't is just trying to survive. There has been so much equity blown away in the last 12 months it's unbelievable. Eatonfield meanwhile continues to make plans; we're just about to become registered as a builder of social housing which will add one more string to our bow.

In today's economic climate pure developers are hurting the most but Eatonfield is a diverse company with a varied portfolio. We've got residential housing, income deals, brownfield sites and leisure all part of our business which has helped us to survive. We've also reacted quickly to market conditions; we've made 50 staff redundant since 2008, we've downsized our offices, completed our residential developments and made a decision not to start any new ones. We've also discounted heavily; the last detached residential property on the market we sold for £300k, down from £399k but that was one house that owed us nothing; we'd already made a good profit on the land.

It's true that none of the banks are lending at the moment but we've been told that as soon as the money is available we'll be top of the pile because Eatonfield is good in this market. This time the situation is very different from the property crash of 1973-4 or 1992-3. This is bigger and deeper, a worldwide recession and one that no-one knows where it's headed or when it's going to end. But I'm still looking to the future, considering partnering deals for example, with capital providers putting up the money and Eatonfield taking the debt. It's important to think creatively, even aggressively, and that's what we're doing, then in the next three to five years I know that Eatonfield will be able to raise the bar once more. I want us to be working with banks to finish off schemes, going for closed deals and building to order. We won't be building speculatively but we will be going back into the investment market for income as we are now seeing double digit yields for the first time in a long time.

At Eatonfield we have credibility because we're a trustworthy company with a good track record and a professional management team. We also have a pipeline of deals that I keep revisiting, looking for discounts and, of course, checking for that one deal that I can 'nick'. I haven't bought anything for 12 months, but by mid 2009 I'm convinced that Eatonfield will be able to start cherry picking again.

On 2nd April 2009 we made a statement announcing that the Eatonfield Group plc had received a resolution to grant outline planning consent for the development plans on our 87 acre Corus site in Cumbria. This was what we had been waiting for and I was delighted; it showed the continued strength of Eatonfield's team in working with local authorities to achieve planning permissions within realistic timescales and that's where I believe Eatonfield is second to none. On 7th April our share price rose to 37p, settling back down to 15p 24 hours later. We then made a subsequent statement saying that we were satisfied that we had previously informed the market of all information of a price-sensitive nature although it was clear that the market considered us undervalued.

I think the secret of my life, if there is one, has been in believing in my goals and taking chances and opportunities when they've been presented to me. That's what I wanted to do with everyone I met in Belfast and that's what I want to do for J, Jo and Dan. And once you've grabbed that opportunity with both hands, remember to have faith in yourself and never give up. It's difficult sometimes, but it's worked for me.

I've never been frightened to take risks in business but even though I've made a bit of money I think I'm the same person as the boy growing up on Nook Farm in the 60s. I'm still the boy at Rydal of whom teachers said: *'if industry were the only criteria for success, he would surely pass';* I'm still the boy in the show jumping ring who went flat out for the clear round and I'm still the boy who idolised his dad. I am pleased that I now have a fantastic relationship with my mother and speak to her everyday, and hope one day she will move back to Cheshire, closer to home.

If I have any regrets it's that I haven't spent more time with my family but what is so amazing is that they all seem to want to spend time with me and what more could a man want?

Well, since you ask, there is just one thing. If you wouldn't mind taking a look at my ambitions for a final time - the ones I came up with at the age of 19 -you'll see there is just one I haven't managed to achieve:

To run a profitable business
To be a millionaire
To marry a beautiful woman
To own a house with a long drive and a snooker room
To send my children to public school
To drive a Bentley
To stay in the best hotels in the world
To own my own racing yard
To give something back by donating to charity
To train a Grand National winner

That elusive Grand National winner could be some way off yet, but it feels like a very good ambition to leave till last. As Sam would say to anyone who'd listen: "He never gives up, does Rob."

INDEX

Running a business the size of Eatonfield would not have been possible without the support of business colleagues, my family and friends and, of course, financial institutions. With this in mind I would like to say 'thank you' to the following people:

Kevin Cassidy, Bobby Bennett and Christine Wardle at AIB, Pat Quinlivan at Bank of Ireland, Steve Ossett at NatWest, Kevin Dunn at RBS, Julian Naylor at Anglo Irish, Andy Teale at Co-op Bank, Wyn Jones and Steve Blake at HSBC, Andy Thomas and James Gaskell at Rothchilds, John Picton at Principality, Terry Reddington at Yorkshire Bank, Jill Jones, Graham Bond, Jan Bailey, Mike Baker, Graham Garner Jones and Gary Potts at Baker Tilly Accountants, David Armitage and Chris Caufield corporate lawyers at Hammonds, Joanne Lake at Evolution and Simon Brown (now at Matrix) of Eatonfield Securities, Chris Bagley of Bridging Finance, Laurie Hoffman EXCEL Securities, John Price at Coutts, Barry Owen, Brendan Flood, Andrew Stewart, Ed Jenner and Gary Lingard, Peter Stevenson, Richard Baddiley, Kevin McLeod aka Mac, Roger Davies of J J Morris, Ron Lloyd, John Taylor, Keith and Colin Bevan, Paul Williams, Nicola and Mandy Smith and my great friends, Eileen and Terry Washer.

Eatonfield would not be the company it is without the support of loyal colleagues Keith Mather, Phil Middlehurst, Steve Hopwood, Ian Arnott, Steve Jones and Moi Jones. Thanks also to Sir Leslie Young and Suki Kalirai, Medwyn Roberts of Impact Communications, Mark Baker of Wilsons Commercial, Mike King at Grimley's and both Dave Lloyd and Mark Scott at Wise Monkey Design and Media. A thank you to all external professional advisors who have helped Eatonfield along the way, and to the Eatonfield Shareholders. To the remaining people at Eatonfield. Special thanks also to Terry Carroll for helping us through the AIM float and to David Armitage, Head of International at Hammonds LLP in Leeds for his continued professional advice.

For all their help with Rob Lloyd Racing I would like to thank, first and foremost, my trainer, Pat Morris, as well as Bobby O'Ryan, Chris O'Donnell, Brian Burrows, David Pickering, Michael Green, Lisa Williamson, Mike Cattermole at Channel 4 racing, Ger Lyons, Eammon Mcullen at Irish Thoroughbred Marketing, Hywel Jones at Jones Digital

Media, Henry and Harry Beeby, Tina and Andrea at Pink Ladies, C & C Catering Ltd, Nick Hancock, Kerry Katona and Mark Fearnall as well as Lisa and Mario from Big Brother. I would also like to show my appreciation for the Nantwich Vetinary Group and Paul Smith our reliable farrier.

For Channel 4's the *Secret Millionaire* I would like to thank everyone at RDF Media and Andrew Mulvenna at his hair salon in Belfast.

I couldn't have done any of this without the support of my family; my mother, Pamela, my Aunty Gill, cousin Paula and Uncle Frank Banner. Thanks also to my children, J, Jo and Dan and to my patient and long-suffering wife, Helen.

Finally, I would like to thank Philip Jordan for the hours spent researching my life, reading everything from school reports to business reports in the process, and to Helen Parker for writing it up into book form.

ROB LLOYD RACING

Things to do

1/ Get C & C sponsors down
2/ Invite Chris Redderton Castle to yard
3/ Spk to Graham Green - Racing Post
4/ " " Ralph Johnston - Daily Express
5/ Sort Web site urgently
6/ Check with Pat - Horse Dentist
7/ Runners for the week
8/ Spk to potential new owners for Breeze ups
9/ See when Bobby is coming
10/ New horses for celeb's   Kerry Katona
                             Nick Hancock
                             Mario v Lisa BBQ
                             + footballers weekend

11/ meeting with Kenry @ Gotts
12/ get store to move Highland Cattle
13/ Check progress with Moi - vineyard
14/ Big Tidy up for Syndicate wkend
15/ Things to do - PAT Staff   clients
                       discipline Suppliers
                       any issues H & S

16/ Re jig ferrier to early wed morning
17/ filming next Friday
18/ Order more jackets for Shop
19/ Make sure Jamie Spencer gets booked for Teddys
                                            Owner

20/ Michael Green wants to see Green Spirit FRI AM
21/ David Prokoving coming with guests on SAT.